The St…
57th (East Surrey) … t,
Royal Artillery (T.A.)

Part One: Conversion and Confrontation, 1938 - 1940

(with a brief account of its predecessors and the 5th East Surreys between the wars)

Ray Goodacre

Privately Printed

Also available in this series:
With the Fighting Cock and the Black Cat in India and Burma:
A History of 82nd Anti-Tank Regiment (and 82nd Light
Anti-Aircraft/Anti-Tank Regiment) Royal Artillery, 1941-1945

Main cover illustration courtesy of the Imperial War Museum, London
Negative number NYP 68075

Published by Ray Goodacre, 7 Eastgate
Banstead, Surrey SM7 1RN

ISBN 978-0-9555780-0-7

Contents | **Page**

Appendices

LIST OF ILLUSTRATIONS

LIST OF MAPS

Introduction and Acknowledgements

This book is the second to appear in a series that sets out to record the story of the 57th (East Surrey) Anti-Tank Regiment, Royal Artillery and its associated units. The history of the war-raised 82nd Anti-Tank Regiment and its campaign in Burma was published in 2002 and the intention is to also produce an account of the second line unit, the 67th (East Surrey) Anti-Tank Regiment.

Chronologically this volume should have been the first to appear as it tells the story of the parent regiment from its formation in 1938, through to the conclusion of the campaign in France and Flanders. It also includes a brief account of the Regiment's predecessor units and a chapter on the 5th East Surreys in the inter-war years, to give some idea of the activities and character of the Territorials who formed the original personnel of the new anti-tank regiment.

My foremost thanks go to the late Colonel Tom Robinson who gave approval for the project to go ahead and was ever generous with information and encouragement. Also to Bob Bradley, whose original research into his father's experiences as an officer with the Regiment was instrumental in the decision to write a history. We made a number of trips together to France and Belgium following in the Regiment's footsteps and Bob also proofread the draft text and provided many helpful comments.

Once again I am indebted to Jack Parkinson, former Honorary Secretary of the 57th/67th Anti-Tank Regiment Old Comrades Association, for giving me access to the membership and for the unfailing help he gave up to his untimely death.

Many former members of the Regiment and their families responded to the various appeals for information and I am hugely grateful to everyone who completed questionnaires, sent written accounts, gave recorded interviews and loaned photographs and other documents. With the length of time that has elapsed since the events took place and with many of the participants no longer with us, it sometimes proved difficult to produce a coherent narrative and without this generous input the job would have been immeasurably harder and the end result poorer.

While it is perhaps invidious to single out one source, I must mention Philip Hampton's detailed account of 228 Battery, which is particularly valuable as it was written only a few months after the events it describes. I am therefore greatly indebted to his son George Hampton who allowed me to reproduce passages from it and also to the Churchill Archives in Cambridge where I first saw it.

I would also like to thank: Mrs Anne Cullis for allowing me to use extracts from the letters of her husband Mervyn Edwards and for her frequent hospitality; the late Joe Courtney who kindly allowed me to use extracts from his privately produced memoir 'Ubique'; Harry Travers for background on his father Lieut-Col R.L. Travers OBE; Penny James, former curator of the Queen's Royal Surrey Regiment Museum at Clandon, for access to archival material; Dr J-P Deweer, Hon. Lt. Col. M.D., for sharing his knowledge on the battle of Oudenarde and for also bringing to my attention the history of the German 30th Infantry Division, a copy of the relevant section from this book was kindly supplied by the Bundesarchiv in Freiburg; Louise Oliver of the Imperial War Museum for permission to reproduce some of its photographs; and the Commonwealth War Graves Commission for providing much of the information on the Regiment's casualties.

For general background on the campaign, I relied most heavily on Gregory Blaxland's excellent Destination Dunkirk and I am grateful to his daughter Lucy Markes for permission to reproduce some extracts from it. I also appreciate the permission of Robert Hale Limited to reproduce the extract from In Durance Vile by John Brown.

The maps that appear in the book are an amalgam of those previously published in the official and regimental histories and I am grateful to their original compilers. The ones of Oudenarde and the Forest of Nieppe also draw on the original War Office maps used by Colonel Robinson in the campaign.

For non-military readers there is a brief chapter at the end of the book that provides some explanation of the organisation and equipment of an anti-tank regiment of the period and its place in the military hierarchy.

On the production side, I would like to thank Michael Bevington of Bespoke Designs who artworked the maps and handled the text layout and design of the book.

In closing, I would most of all like to thank my wife Nancy and children Sophie and Natalie for their support over the many years it has taken to bring the book to completion. Nancy's proofreading and occasional gentle editing with a fresh eye also helped to make the text more readable. Any errors though are of course mine alone.

The book is dedicated to all members of the Regiment and their families, past and present, and especially to those men who did not return.

Ray Goodacre
Bookham, Surrey
March 2007

Officers of the Streatham Detachment in the late 1880s

PREFACE

Early Days

In the years between the two world wars the British Army experienced a period of great technological upheaval as it adapted to wholesale mechanisation and the significant developments of the First World War. Many changes in organisation and armament took place and for many units it meant the loss of their traditional roles.

The tank was first used in action by the British Army on the Somme in 1916 and its success in breaking the deadlock of trench warfare and restoring the possibility of manoeuvre to the battlefield proved a decisive factor in the eventual Allied victory. Though much thought and training was given thereafter to the problem of providing an effective system of anti-tank defence for the infantry, it was not until very late in the preparatory period before the Second World War that specialised anti-tank units appeared equipped with the purpose-designed 2-pounder anti-tank gun. Five regular field artillery regiments were converted to the new role in 1938 and ten similar conversions were carried out in the Territorial Army.

Among the latter was the 5th Battalion The East Surrey Regiment, an old Territorial Infantry Battalion with its headquarters in Wimbledon, which recruited in Surrey and South West London. The Battalion traced a direct lineage to the Victorian volunteer movement of 1859 that flourished as a result of the growing fears of an invasion by the French under Emperor Napoleon III. Volunteer forces, mostly corps of riflemen, sprang up all over the country, comprised of citizens who were prepared to devote some of their leisure time to military training. Many of the smaller corps were grouped into Administrative Battalions in which they retained their own identities, but combined to ensure uniformity of training.

The 5th Battalion was formed originally as the 1st Adminstrative Battalion Surrey Rifle Volunteer Corps and by 1862 it included the four

Corps that, with slight modification, remained as the recruiting districts. They were the 4th (Brixton), 8th (Carshalton), 11th (Wimbledon) and 25th (Epsom) Corps.[(1)]

In April 1880 the 1st Administrative Battalion was consolidated into a single corps and its title changed to the 4th and subsequently to the 3rd Surrey Rifle Volunteers. Although all the detachments in the Battalion now bore one regimental number, this consolidation caused very little practical change and each detachment continued to have its own drill station and control over its recruiting and finances.

Closer links with the Regular Army were forged as a result of the Cardwell Reforms which combined the Regular Infantry of the Line, Volunteers and Militia on a territorial basis in county regiments. This link was formalised in December 1887 when the 3rd Surrey Rifle Volunteers assumed the title of the 2nd Volunteer Battalion The East Surrey Regiment. The Battalion later changed its rifle green uniforms for the scarlet tunics of the Regiment.

The call to active service came on the outbreak of war between Britain and the Boer republics in South Africa in 1899. The Battalion provided detachments for a Volunteer Service Company and to the City Imperial Volunteers. On arrival in South Africa, the Service Company took part in the operations in support of Lord Roberts' advance on Pretoria and later manning the blockhouse lines built to curtail the movements of the Boer commandos.

A surge in recruitment during this period led to the formation of additional detachments in Putney and Leatherhead, of which the former was later transferred to the London area, while the latter remained with the Battalion.

The South African war had demonstrated many military deficiencies, one of them being the need to reorganise and consolidate the various auxiliary and reserve forces then in existence. The result was that under the impetus and guidance of Lord Haldane, Secretary of State for War, the Territorial and Reserve Forces Act was passed, leading to the formation of the Territorial Force in 1908.

The 2nd Volunteer Battalion was formally recognised as a unit of the Territorial Force on 11 June of that year, as the 5th Battalion The East Surrey Regiment. The new force was organised on the same basis as the Regular Army and the Battalion was included in the Surrey Infantry Brigade of the Home Counties Division. Its administration was taken over by the Territorial Force Association of the County of Surrey, while the recruiting area remained as Wimbledon, Streatham, Sutton, Epsom and Leatherhead.

For the first time in their history the volunteer units were permitted to bear Colours and on 19 June 1909 His Majesty King Edward VII presented the King's and Regimental Colours to a party of officers from the Battalion sent to Windsor to receive them. The King's Colour bore the battle honour 'South Africa 1900-1902.'

The Battalion was in annual camp at the outbreak of war in August 1914 and returned immediately to Wimbledon to mobilise and later moved to Canterbury where the Surrey Brigade was concentrating. When orders were received to raise a 'second line' unit the original battalion became known as the 1/5th Battalion The East Surrey Regiment.

On 29 October, the Battalion sailed from Southampton for India, where it was employed on garrison duties at Cawnpore and later several other stations. The Battalion also provided drafts for other units, one of which went to Mesopotamia and sustained heavy casualties in action against the Turks. In November 1917 the whole Battalion was ordered to Mesopotamia and took part in the operations on the River Tigris which resulted in the enemy's final surrender. After the Armistice in November 1918 the Battalion remained with the army of occupation in Mesopotamia and was involved in punitive operations against insurgents in Southern Kurdistan. The Battalion arrived home in February 1920 after more than five years service abroad and demobilisation commenced immediately.

The 2/5th Battalion formed in 1914 was engaged in home defence and the recruitment and training of officers and men in order to provide drafts for other units of The East Surrey Regiment in all the theatres of war. A 3/5th Battalion was also raised in 1915 with a similar recruitment and training role.

NOTES

(1) The Battalion also included at this time the 2nd Corps at Croydon, which gained sufficient strength to become independent in 1867, and the 20th Corps formed at Lower Norwood and apparently disbanded in 1863.

CHAPTER ONE

Soldiering in Peacetime: The 5th East Surreys 1920-1938

At the end of the 1914-18 war the Territorial Force was briefly disbanded, but then reconstituted in February 1920 as the Territorial Army with its status and duties wholly changed. It was now the only source, besides the much reduced Regular Army and its small reserve, from which armed forces could be supplied for the defence of the country.

The 5th Battalion was reformed under the command of Lieutenant-Colonel W.A. Gillett, T.D., who had been Second-in-Command on the outbreak of the war and raised the 2/5th Battalion.

In the aftermath of the war, the country did not regard soldiering with much enthusiasm, but when the Battalion opened for recruiting in April 1920 it grew steadily in numbers and took the lead in the Surrey Brigade. It also had the distinction of being the only unit in the Brigade to go into annual camp at Worthing in August for the full period of 15 days. Although younger men were in the majority, the Battalion contained a fair sprinkling of ex-service men who had re-enlisted in their old unit and, together with the instructors of the permanent staff, formed a nucleus on which the unit was built. The permanent staff included an adjutant, regimental sergeant major and four instructors from the Regular Battalions. The camp proved a great stimulus to recruiting, and within a week or two after its conclusion the strength was almost doubled to 230. So well did the new recruits come forward that it was decided to hold a second camp for the new men, and in September the camping ground at Worthing was again visited by the Battalion.

The work of reconstructing the Battalion moved ahead rapidly thereafter, with week-night training put in at the various drill halls. The headquarters and one company were based at St George's Road, Wimbledon and the other companies were at Streatham, Sutton and

Epsom, with a detachment at Leatherhead. A new feature was the formation of a Headquarters Unit, with its various sections – signalling, machine-gun and transport – each under the command of an officer. Everything possible was done to create a good esprit de corps and a good deal of attention was paid to sports and the social side of the men's lives.

In April of the following year, the coal miners came out on strike and the Territorial Army was called upon to assist in forming the new units of the Defence Force to help maintain law and order in case of an emergency. The Battalion had a busy time enlisting men on a 90 days engagement for the 5th Battalion The East Surrey Regiment (Defence Force). Nearly all the officers and a large proportion of men joined and it also attracted a good many members of the old 1/5th Battalion to its ranks, some of whom re-enlisted into the Territorial Army. The Battalion camped in the Home Park, Hampton Court.

A short time after the demobilisation of the Defence Force, all ranks were actively engaged in preparations for the annual training camp to be held at Worthing in August. The strength of the Battalion prior to the camp was 22 officers and 304 men.

Gradually the yearly calendar returned to its peace-time pattern as one by one the familiar activities and institutions were revived. The Band made its first public appearance at the unveiling of the Wimbledon War Memorial on the common on 5 November 1921, at which a party of the 5th Battalion were present under Captain B.D. Ogden, M.C. Four senior non-commissioned officers (NCOs) were stationed at the four corners of the monument and buglers of the Battalion sounded the Last Post and Reveille at appropriate moments. The proceedings were watched by a huge crowd.

In May 1922 Colonel E. Horsman Bailey, V.D., T.D., retired as Honorary Colonel and the Battalion welcomed as his successor Colonel R.K. Harvey, T.D., who had been associated with the Battalion and its predecessor unit in the Volunteer Force since 1886. He commanded it at the outbreak of war and took it overseas to India in 1914.

A most important event, the annual prize distribution, was held for the first time since the war at the headquarters, Wimbledon, in January 1923 and much of the enthusiasm which characterised the event in pre-war days once more marked the occasion. The ceremony was presided over by Sir Charles Tyrell Giles who distributed the cups and medals to the winning teams and to individual winners of the shooting, sport and athletics competitions held within the Battalion.

The Commanding Officer, Colonel Gillett, gave an outline of the progress made by the Battalion since its reconstitution. He said the strength had now reached 467 men, but that it had not been an easy task, mainly owing to the great disturbance of thought following the war, and principally to the fact that unemployment was the chief enemy. However he was glad to say that they had now formed the nucleus of a good battalion. They came out top of the Brigade in shooting, and on their strength they were the best battalion in the Division. He also alluded to the happy relations that existed between the Battalion and the Regular Depot of The East Surrey Regiment at Kingston. While the Battalion had seen very little of the Depot and the Regular Battalions before the war, the following years would see the forging of close links and a keen regimental spirit uniting them all.

The command of the Battalion changed in 1924 with Lieutenant-Colonel G.B. Chetwynd-Stapylton succeeding Colonel Gillett.

A new drill hall station was opened at Walton-on-the-Hill in 1926, bringing in 20 new recruits to augment C Company at Sutton. The following year, many overdue improvements were made to the old drill hall at Wimbledon (opened in 1879) including the addition of a men's club room.

In 1929, the New Year found B Company at Wimbledon undergoing a transformation from a rifle to a machine gun company, in accordance with the reorganisation of Territorial battalions into three rifle companies and one machine-gun company.

The command of the Battalion changed again on 9 April 1930, when Lieutenant-Colonel W.H. Hatchard-Smith succeeded Colonel

Chetwynd-Stapylton. Colonel Hatchard-Smith commanded the Battalion during a period of rising unemployment and when financial stringency reached its peak. These were very difficult times for the Territorial Army with camps cancelled and training grants cut.

With numbers and interest diminishing, great efforts were made to liven up recruiting. At the request of the Lord Lieutenant of the County, a recruiting committee had been formed at Wimbledon in 1926 to assist the officers to bring the detachment up to strength. In 1930 the committee extended its scope to embrace the Battalion as a whole with detachment committees formed at Sutton, Epsom and Leatherhead. The Peace Establishment of a Territorial Infantry Battalion was 604, but the strength of the Battalion at the end of the year had fallen to only 393.

The committee felt that the best way to stimulate recruitment was to make service in the Battalion as attractive as possible and appealed to the local community for financial support. An annual income of £500 was needed to supplement the governmental grants, which were insufficient to meet the necessary annual expenditure on such requirements as extra ammunition, sports equipment, prizes for shooting, maintenance of the Band and Drums and entertainments.

Recruiting weeks and marches were held throughout the Battalion area with the Band and Drums parading or leading a march of the local company before large numbers of spectators. The Band and Drums were now completely equipped with scarlet uniform provided by the recruiting committee. Sir William Wells, chairman of the executive recruiting committee, also presented a handsome Drum Major's Staff.

New recruits were required to enlist for four years and at the end of that period could re-engage for a further one, two, three or four years. The minimum training required of a recruit in his first year was to attend 40 'drills', to fire the annual range course and 15 days (or a minimum of eight days) attendance at camp. In the second and subsequent years the men were obliged to attend twenty 'drills'. An annual bounty of £5 was offered for those completing the training and the men received pay at camp, with a Private commanding a daily rate of two shillings.

In 1932, owing to the financial crisis, recruiting was restricted and with only limited funds the annual training was reduced to a voluntary week at Bisley during the last week of July.

The next year's improved financial conditions enabled the resumption of normal annual training and the Battalion settled down to its yearly routine which followed a familiar pattern.

Shooting occupied a good deal of attention, with Sunday visits to the ranges at Westcott near Dorking and voluntary camps at Westcott and Bisley held during the Easter and Whitsun holidays. A prize rifle meeting was held each year and the Battalion competed in the Territorial Army Rifle Association competitions and Surrey County Rifle Meetings among others. During the winter months, when training moved indoors, attention focused on the inter-detachment miniature range competition.

The annual training usually took place at the end of July or the beginning of August and lasted for 15 days. The Battalion camped with its fellow East Surrey Territorials, the 6th Battalion, and the two Territorial Battalions of The Queen's Royal West Surrey Regiment in 131st Infantry Brigade. Attendance at camp always received a boost when it was arranged at a seaside location, where the men could spend their off duty time as they would a summer holiday. Popular sites visited during the inter-war years included Arundel, Seaford, Shoreham, Shorncliffe and Worthing. A progressive training programme was arranged, starting with simple section work, going on through platoon and company exercises to battalion training, and winding up with a brigade field day in the second week. The Battalion also competed in the military and athletics sports competitions held at camp in which it was usually well placed.

In addition to the annual prize giving, the two principal social events of the winter season were the Sergeants' Annual New Year Dance and, noisiest of all, the Children's Christmas Party.

There was sport in its season including football, cricket, cross country and athletics. One of the highlights was the Inter-Unit sports meeting held at the Depot, where the units of The East Surrey Regiment competed for the Hood cup. The Battalion won this cup in 1923 and 1930.

The Battalion boxing championships took place at Wimbledon usually in February. The winners went on to compete in the Brigade competitions and by winning the finals of their weights, qualified to represent the Brigade in the Divisional Competition.

There was still time and occasions for ceremonial activities including detachments at civil occasions, church parades and Remembrance Sunday, when the Battalion paraded at Wimbledon and marched in the procession to the War Memorial carrying its colours and accompanied by the Band and Drums.

All these activities were in addition to the ordinary week-night training at the drill halls. So the years passed for the Battalion.

In April 1934 Lieutenant-Colonel B.D. Ogden, M.C., was appointed to command the Battalion on the retirement of Colonel Hatchard-Smith. In the summer, a new drill hall at Leatherhead was officially opened by Lord Ashcombe, the Lord Lieutenant of Surrey, who was received by a Guard of Honour, under the command of Captain C.F. Masters. The new hall was excellently designed and equipped both for military and social purposes, with a modern miniature range and good club room.

The Battalion took part in three celebrations in connection with the Silver Jubilee of HM King George V in 1935. On Jubilee Day a carnival march was organised by the Borough of Wimbledon and on the following Sunday a Mass Service of Thanksgiving was held on the All England Tennis Grounds. Both these parades were well attended. At Epsom the celebration took the form of a Searchlight Tattoo, in which the Battalion provided most of the items in the programme.

The same year Colonel W.A. Gillett vacated the appointment of Honorary Colonel of the Battalion and Lord Ebbisham, a former officer of the Sutton Detachment, consented to succeed him.

Marching to Annual Camp, Shorncliffe 1936

The Officers at Wimbledon 1936 [1]

In 1936 the annual camp was at Shorncliffe, near the 2nd Battalion The East Surrey Regiment stationed at Risborough Barracks. Never before had the Battalion had an opportunity of lying next to one of the Regular battalions, and the close liaison between the two units for two weeks aroused in all ranks a very strong Regimental spirit. The vicinity of Folkestone, Hythe and Sandgate also made Shorncliffe a popular spot and attendance was very good

After camp, Captain P.H. Drake-Brockman, from the 2nd Battalion, succeeded Captain A.L. Sutton, M.C., as Adjutant.

In November, the Right Hon. A. Duff Cooper, Secretary of State for War, presented the prizes at the Annual Prize Distribution held on this occasion at Wimbledon Town Hall. The next month saw the Battalion assisting in the ceremony of the proclamation of King George VI with parades at Sutton and Wimbledon.(2)

While the routine of peace-time soldiering continued for the Battalion, the uneasy international situation in Europe gave warning that the chance of a war was again probable. The importance of the Territorial Army became more evident, equipment began to come through more readily and there was much reorganisation and belated modernisation.

In early 1937 orders were received that the Battalions of The East Surrey Regiment were to change from a rifle to a machine-gun role. B (Support) Company in Wimbledon, which it will be recalled had converted in 1929, set about imparting its knowledge of the Vickers machine gun to the other companies. Machine gun instructors were sent round to each detachment in turn with A Company in Streatham the first to commence conversion.

Another important change was that in a re-organisation of the Territorial Infantry Brigades, the Battalion, along with the 6th East Surreys, left 131st Infantry Brigade and joined the 23rd London (East Surrey) Regiment and the 5th The Queens Royal West Kent Regiment to form the 132nd Infantry Brigade in 44th Division.

The main interest in the months before camp this year was the

Coronation of King George VI. Amongst other local activities, the Battalion was represented in London by three officers and twenty five men who took part in lining the streets and in the actual Coronation Procession.

The camp at Arundel Park was spent with their new companions in 132nd Brigade and all enjoyed a splendid fortnight with beautiful weather. For the first time the Battalion was provided with motor trucks which were of immense value both as administrative and fighting vehicles.

In December the prizes were presented by no less a distinguished officer than General Sir W. Edmund Ironside, the future Chief of the Imperial General Staff. In his report, the Commanding Officer mentioned that the strength of the Battalion was then greater than it had been for a long time with 21 Officers and 385 men.

In the new year, orders came for The East Surrey Regiment to change back from machine gun battalions to rifle battalions. The news was received with some disappointment and much that had been done in the past months had to be undone. The new organisation for an infantry battalion was four rifle companies and a headquarter company. It was accompanied by new tactics and the issue of new equipment in the shape of the Bren light machine gun and Boys anti-tank rifle, although both were in short supply. Officers and senior NCOs were introduced to the new tactics at the Easter camp at Bisley where there was a record attendance. At the same time the whole Battalion was introduced to the new Field Drill of marching in three ranks rather than four.

On 9 April 1938, Colonel Ogden retired and Lieutenant-Colonel J.A. Imison, M.C., became Commanding Officer. Colonel Imison had nearly twenty three years' service to his credit, all in The East Surrey Regiment. He joined the 3/5th Battalion as a Second-Lieutenant in 1915, and later took part in some of the heaviest fighting of the war in France and Flanders while attached, first to the 23rd London Regiment and afterwards to the 1st Battalion. His gallantry and able leadership earned him the Military Cross, and later a bar to the decoration. He was wounded at Messines in June 1917. Upon reconstruction of the Territorial Army in 1920 Colonel Imison returned to duty with the 5th Battalion. Like his predecessor he was a schoolmaster. Major F.W.C. Hill took over the duties of Second-in-Command of the Battalion.

The annual training at Falmer was a camp of many new ideas and practices, and possibly for this reason, coupled with its close proximity to Brighton and good weather, it proved to be one of the most popular and well attended camps for many years. For the first time, gas masks were a personal issue, and during the whole training period conditions as near as possible to those to be expected on active service were observed. Training was given on the Bren gun and new two-inch mortar, the new Field Drill came into full operation and the air and gas alarms raised from time to time in the camp area gave excellent practice.

Every effort was made to stimulate recruiting and by September the strength of the Battalion passed the 400 mark, but this was still well below establishment.

The situation in Europe was very grave at this time with war looming over the German threat to Czechoslovakia for the return of the Sudentenland. The Nazi Party had assumed power in Germany in 1933 and this latest act of belligerency followed its reoccupation of the Rhineland in 1936 and the annexation of Austria earlier in 1938. The British Prime Minister, Neville Chamberlain, held a series of meetings with Adolf Hitler which ended with an agreement at Munich on 30 September. War was averted only by ceding to Germany's demands, but Britain had bought some more time in which to gather strength.

Although the Battalion was not mobilised during the crisis, many officers and men came to the various drill halls and much enthusiastic and voluntary work was put in. Captain D.H. Chapman and Lance Corporal W.J. Pryse were also employed as Staff Captain and Brigade Clerk at 132nd Brigade Headquarters.

As the year drew to a close the Battalion looked back on a period of constant changes and thought that they had adapted to them with some success. Some of the changes had been anticipated, but there was another change to come which they did not expect.

NOTES

(1) Caption: (back row left to right) Lt D.H. Chapman, 2/Lt L.B. Chapman, Lt P.J.W. Wells, Lt R.H. Hatton, 2/Lt V.C.C. Owen, 2/Lt P.G. Hampton, 2/Lt G.S. Abbott, 2/Lt N.R.A. Crowe, Lt D.G. Grugeon, 2/Lt N.C. Westwood; (front row left to right) Capt O.P. Partridge, Capt C.F. Masters, Major F.W.C. Hill, Major J.A. Imison, Lt Col B.D. Ogden, Capt A.L. Sutton, Capt M.H. Prance, Capt T.H. Willoughby, Capt (QM) F.W. Grogan.

(2) This was the second time in the same year that the Battalion had participated in the ceremony of the proclamation of a new monarch following the accession of Edward VIII in January. On his abdication eleven months later he was succeeded by his brother King George VI.

CHAPTER 2

A Change of Role

Rumours of pending changes were in the air soon after the Munich crisis had passed, but there was little to suggest that in a few short weeks the Battalion would be transferred into a completely new arm. Official intimation was received in November, however, that it would adopt the new role of an Anti-Tank Regiment Royal Artillery by the 28th of that month.[(1)]

Before assuming its new mantle the Battalion enjoyed one last formal function as East Surreys – the Annual Prize Distribution at Wimbledon on 8th December. The Secretary of State for War, Lesley Hore-Belisha, attended the event and in his speech naturally referred to the transition. He said that among the new types of unit which were being developed to meet the modern demands was the Anti-Tank Regiment. 'Famous infantry battalions, like your own,' he said, 'are thus invited to assume another task – a task which will demand all your application and all those energies which you have hitherto devoted to your work in the line.'

A contemporary account of the change appeared in *The Journal of the East Surrey Regiment,* in which the 5th Battalion notes were published throughout the inter-war years: 'The news was received with mixed feelings – on the one hand relief that the unit would remain part of the Field Army (there had been some talk of a change over to Searchlights), and on the other hand deep regret on leaving The East Surrey Regiment, with which the Battalion had been associated for fifty one years.

'Military requirements, however, take little account of sentiment, and when the change came all ranks, like the good soldiers they are, proceeded to get on with the job. The Regiment is quickly settling down after the violent upheaval, and with the arrival of two new 2-pounder anti-tank guns and four trucks has got down to really intensive training.

The Adjutant and Permanent Staff Instructors attended anti-tank gun courses at Aldershot as soon as the changeover had taken place, and in an incredibly short time all the number ones of the Regiment were fully trained in their duties as instructors in gun drill and laying.'

The breaking away from old Regimental associations was naturally acutely felt by the older generation of officers and men, but given the options of joining the Royal Artillery, transferring to another infantry battalion or a complete discharge, in the main there was a consensus to stick together and make the best of it. To preserve a link with the past, a successful application was later made to the War Office that the title 'East Surrey' be incorporated in its new designation as the 57th Anti-Tank Regiment Royal Artillery (T.A.).

The various alterations necessitated by the change of role were as follows:

A Company (Streatham) became 225 Anti-Tank Battery with A, B and C Troops

B Company (Wimbledon) became 226 Anti-Tank Battery with D, E and F Troops

C Company (Sutton) became 227 Anti-Tank Battery with G, H and I Troops

D Company (Epsom and Leatherhead) became 228 Anti-Tank Battery with J, K and L Troops

Unfortunately the Walton-on-the-Hill Detachment ceased to exist, mainly owing to the difficulty in hiring a village hall large enough to accommodate one of the 2-pounder guns and for drills. In the circumstances Colonel Imison was reluctantly compelled to close down this old detachment.

Another effect of the changeover was the loss of the Band and Drums, but it was hoped to absorb the personnel into the new establishment which did include the provision of nine trumpeters. The Band and Drums would also continue to arise phoenix-like on a number of occasions in the future.

By the close of 1938, the strength of the Regiment had increased to 27

Wimbledon - the first 2-pounder anti-tank guns

Annual Camp, Tilshead, August 1939

officers and 466 other ranks, but fifty more recruits were still needed to bring the batteries up to full strength.

In addition to the two new 2-pounders received, six further anti-tank guns were promised by the late spring. The arrival of these additional weapons was anxiously awaited, since the task of training 450 men at five different drill halls with only two guns was beyond human prowess. On War Office paper an anti-tank regiment consisted of a headquarters and four batteries each of 12 anti-tank guns. The batteries were divided into three troops each of four guns, and a troop into two sections of two guns. With the 2-pounder in short supply, however, the batteries were fortunate if they saw more than a couple of guns in the coming months and to begin with the training required a good deal of imagination.

As its name suggests, the 2-pounder anti-tank gun was specifically designed to pierce the armour of tanks and other armoured fighting vehicles. It was a direct-fire weapon (i.e. the target is visible from the gun) firing a shell of high velocity with a flat trajectory. Its effective range was 2000 yards, but better results could be expected at 800 yards or less. Training focused on the natural tendency to fire too soon and too fast, which also prematurely disclosed the position of the gun, but the opportunities for firing practice with live 2-pounder ammunition were few and far between. The gun was mounted on a low carriage with two wheels that could be quickly removed to enable the carriage to be lowered onto three legs for the normal firing method. Where time permitted a gun emplacement would be dug and the position concealed. In the case of an emergency, the gun could be fired from off its wheels, but the traverse was limited due to the main shield fouling the wheels.

An individual gun detachment consisted of five men each allocated a number and with clearly defined duties as laid down in the drill book. The Number One, holding the rank of sergeant or bombardier, was in charge of the crew. It was his responsibility to select the target and direct the gun onto it, to decide when and at what range to open fire, and to observe the path of shot and indicate adjustments. The Number Two was the loader and he would kneel at the right-hand side of the breech and push the round home, reloading thereafter as soon as the gun had been fired. The Number Three sat on the gun layer's seat and fired the gun on orders by pressing the trigger pedal with his left foot. He used a telescopic sight to make fine adjustments when aiming the gun and to follow moving targets, also using a traversing handwheel. Numbers Four and Five were the ammunition numbers who were responsible for maintaining the supply of ammunition to the gun and were available to replace casualties. A detachment also included the driver of the gun-tower. The drill to unhook the gun from the tower and bring it into action on its platform, using a handspike to lift the left and right legs while the wheels were removed, was practiced ceaselessly and against the clock. Each member of a gun crew was expected to be able to do every job and the order to 'change round' was a regular feature of the drill.

In addition to training everyone as gunners, as an anti-tank regiment was completely mechanized, the Regiment was also faced with the task of training half the men as drivers. The few available Morris 15 hundredweight gun towers and 8 hundredweight utility trucks were used for carrying out driving instruction, but the number of men holding civilian licences were in the minority. Men interested in motor vehicles were urgently needed, especially those with any knowledge of fitters' duties and who were offered promotion on their mechanical ability alone.

Minor alterations were carried out at all the drill halls except Epsom to enable the trucks and guns to be manoeuvred in and out and additional garage accommodation was acquired. For many years the Regiment had been trying to convince the authorities that its various drill halls required improving and modernising and with money now being made available at long last things began to happen. A few years back a new drill hall had been built in Leatherhead and now Streatham was entirely rebuilt and enlarged. It was officially declared open by the Mayor of Wandsworth on a wet night in January 1939. There were also high hopes that the derelict hall at Epsom, the moribund one at Sutton and, last but not least, the overcrowded one at Wimbledon might receive some attention.[(2)]

On the international scene, March 1939 saw the occupation of the remains of Czechoslovakia by Germany and a hardening of the position of the British Government. A guarantee of aid was given to Poland, which seemed most likely to be the next victim of German aggression. The Government announced that the Territorial Army would be doubled and barely a month later conscription was re-introduced.

While these momentous events were taking place, the Regiment spent the best part of the Easter holiday on Chobham Ridges, where, for the first time since the change, they put a full-strength battery with guns and vehicles 'on the floor'. The training was carried out with the greatest enthusiasm with 28 officers and more than 150 men taking part in the exercises.

During the week of the announcement of conscription, recruits came in at such a rate that the headquarters and drill halls found difficulty in coping with the number of attestations. At Wimbledon, applicants were dealt with until five minutes before midnight on Wednesday 26 April and more than 50 signed the necessary forms. Among the old Territorials there was scepticism that these new recruits were motivated by exemption from conscription, but in fairness many of the men who enlisted at this time, realising that they would be drafted, preferred to be in a local unit of their choice and among friends.

With the Regiment brought up to its war establishment of 540 officers and men, recruiting continued apace for the 'doubling up' of the unit and by early May it was one of the first units in Surrey to report its second line complete. With both units sharing the existing drill halls and training taking place most nights, there was much overcrowding and various measures were taken to acquire temporary accommodation. For the new recruits the drills to begin with were just that – foot drill. There being insufficient small arms for rifle drill, or 2-pounder anti guns for gun-drill, they formed threes and marched up and down the street alongside the halls.

The new unit, designated the 67th Anti-Tank Regiment Royal Artillery (T.A.), was officially formed on 1 June with its Headquarters at Wimbledon, 265 Battery at Streatham, 266 Battery at Wimbledon, 267 Battery at Sutton and 268 Battery at Streatham, although men from Wimbledon, Epsom and Leatherhead were posted to the latter.(3) Major F.W.C. Hill, T.D., was appointed as Commanding Officer. While new recruits were in the majority, a number of experienced NCOs from the 57th were posted to carry out training in the new Regiment. This separation was keenly felt by these men, who almost overnight lost friendships formed during the pre-war years.

At the end of the month, members of both Regiments took part in a Torchlight Tattoo at Wimbledon Stadium. The Band and Drums once again donned their scarlet uniforms and the old colours of the 5th East Surreys were paraded.(4) On one of the evenings, Sir Malcolm Fraser, the newly appointed Lord Lieutenant of the County, took the salute and inspected a guard of honour under the command of Major T.H. Willoughby.

During this period, new officers with gunner credentials arrived to share their knowledge. They included Warrant Officers of the Royal Artillery given emergency commissions and former Cadets from the school and college Officer Training Corps who had then served in the ranks of Territorial gunner units like the 98th Field Regiment (Surrey and Sussex Yeomanry Q.M.R.).

In August, the two Regiments went to Tilshead on Salisbury Plain for a fortnight's annual training. Although they camped together, the individual Regiments paraded, drilled and trained separately. The camp mustered 900 men and with a general feeling that war was coming, it was a serious and hard working affair. The training took on a sense of urgency and for the first time the 2-pounder guns were fired 'live' on the ranges. At the end of each day all the brass shell cases had to be retrieved and accounted for, then cleaned, polished and greased for re-use. For the new recruits, some of whom were without uniform, the camp gave them their first taste of Army life. While the first week was wet and overcast, a hot and sunny second week was not without its lighter moments with strong cider sampled.

When camp broke up on 20 August, there were many who thought that they were fortunate to be going home, unlike their fathers in the 5th East Surreys who had returned immediately to Wimbledon to mobilise on the outbreak of war in 1914.

NOTES

(1) Authority: War Office letter 20/Arty./5347 (T.A.I.) dated 16 November, 1938.

(2) The drill hall at Epsom was demolished in April 1940.

(3) Authority: War Office letter 20/Arty/5492 (T.A.I) dated 1 June 1939. Approval was also given later to include the title 'East Surrey' in its designation.

The provisional distribution of the two Regiments recommended to the War Office was for the first line with its headquarters and two batteries at Wimbledon and two batteries at Streatham, while the second line would have its headquarters and two batteries at Sutton and additional batteries at Epsom and Leatherhead. The final distribution was no doubt influenced by the number of men who enlisted in each of the recruiting areas, in which Streatham took the lead.

(4) A Regiment of the Royal Artillery does not carry colours, its guns are its colours.

CHAPTER 3

The Outbreak of War

As the summer of 1939 drew to a close and Germany pressed ahead with its plans to attack Poland, war appeared inevitable. In expectation, the Regimental key parties were called up on 24 August and reported to the drill halls to prepare for embodiment. This involved making the necessary arrangements for the reception, equipping, feeding and accommodation of the men.

The German offensive on Poland opened at dawn on 1 September. Great Britain at once ordered full mobilisation and mindful of its guarantee to Poland sent an ultimatum to Germany to withdraw its troops. The telephone order for the Regiment to embody was received at Wimbledon at 4.30 p.m. and relayed immediately to the other batteries. Officers were contacted by telegram, call-up notices went out by post to the men, and during the afternoon the BBC announced over the radio instructions for all Territorials to report to their units. Hearing the news, the men left their places of work and stopping off at home to pick up their kit made their way to the drill halls. All through the evening they turned up and, with both Regiments embodying, the scenes were somewhat chaotic, but by midnight all batteries had reported considerable progress. As they were now in effect full-time soldiers, the men slept in the drill halls or were billeted locally, while the lucky ones were allowed to return home for the night.

The telegram to mobilise for active service arrived the next morning. Those first few days of the war were a busy time as the batteries sorted themselves out. Medical inspections had to be carried out, equipment issued, forms completed and guards placed on vulnerable points as directed. For their meals the men marched in relays to the local cafes.

On Sunday 3 September, having received no response from Germany, the Prime Minister informed the nation that it was once again at war. Many men heard the news while at morning church parade and shortly after they also heard the air-raid sirens sound the first, false alarm.

The following day the batteries left their individual drill halls to concentrate with Regimental Headquarters at the racecourse on Epsom Downs. Home to the famous Derby, all racing was abandoned for the duration of the war and it was turned over to the military. The Regiment was accommodated in the main grandstand, a large steel and concrete structure with a long climb to the top where the men slept on palliases on the hard stone floor, while the officers were more fortunate in sharing some of the private boxes. The sergeant's mess was established in the nearby Derby Arms public house.

During the first few days great emphasis was placed on Passive Air Defence measures which involved sandbagging, trench digging, blacking out and the manning of anti-aircraft Bren gun posts. The urgency was brought home by an air raid warning, but no aircraft were seen.

The Regiment soon settled down to the routine of military life, with the day governed by trumpet and bugle calls from Reveille in the morning to Last Post at night. The sounding of Reveille was followed by a scramble to get washed, shaved and breakfasted. After which, the day was spent on gun drill, maintenance and driving instruction, and individual training that included foot drill, weapon instruction, gas mask drill and other specialist disciplines like signalling. A new feature of the gun drill was the digging of gun emplacements on the Downs and filling them up again. Toughening up for everyone included physical training on the racecourse, cross-country running and long route marches singing the songs their fathers had sung before them in the last war.

Equipment also started arriving, but was still in short supply and had to be used on a rota basis. The situation was not improved with the handover of some guns and vehicles to 67th Anti-Tank Regiment which had also now moved to the racecourse.[(1)] The shortage of transport was only relieved by impressing civilian vehicles of uncertain mechanical reliability. A transport pool was established in front of the grandstand

The Grandstand, Epsom Racecourse

2-pounder anti-tank gun on Epsom Downs

and later a petrol dump. Guard duties could be eerie on a windy night with the flapping of the loose truck canvasses and buckling of the 'flimsy' petrol cans, due to the changes in temperature, causing nervous sentries to call out the guard.

There were many changes in personnel at this time. On the arrivals side were the partially trained conscripts, or Militiamen as they were termed, and a hundred Reservists, time served soldiers and mostly former NCOs who quickly regained their stripes. On the departures side were the under 19 year-olds, or so called immatures, who left for the 59th Heavy Anti-Aircraft Regiment, Royal Artillery in Essex, and the men only fit for home service who were transferred to the 67th. The end of the month saw the strength of the Regiment at 28 officers and 488 men.

The first phase of training was now coming to an end and on 27 September an advance party left the racecourse to join a divisional column moving to a new training area in Dorset and Somerset. The job of the advance party was to make the arrangements for the Regiment's reception and billeting in the new area. A short leave of seven days was granted to all ranks, some of whom took the opportunity to get married. During the time at Epsom the process of welding the individual batteries into a whole had got underway and the new recruits had experienced the rigours of military discipline, drill and training.

At the same time as the Regiment was preparing to move, the fighting formations of the British Expeditionary Force (BEF) were crossing over to France to take up positions alongside its ally. From fear of German air attack, French ports well to the west had been selected with the main troop landings taking place at Cherbourg and the vehicles and supplies being landed at Brest and Nantes.

On the other side of Europe, Poland had been defeated by Germany only five weeks after the campaign had begun. Although they had put up a brave fight, the Polish forces had been overwhelmed by fast moving armoured formations supported by strong air power. Their fate was sealed when Russia in league with Germany joined in the conflict and invaded the country from the east.

On 20 October the road party with the Regiment's guns and vehicles also left for the new training area. Staging the night at Bulford camp on Salisbury Plain, the party arrived next day at the town of Chard in Somerset having experienced some mechanical trouble en route with its impressed vehicles. The main body of the Regiment marched to Epsom Downs station on the night of the 22nd to move by train to Chard. Arriving the following morning, and leaving 225 Battery billeted in the Dairy at Chard Junction, the Regiment marched into the town while the transport moved back and forth ferrying its baggage.

A variety of buildings were taken over in the town with Regimental Headquarters located in the Drill Hall Cottage on Furnham Road, 228 Battery Headquarters in the Drill Hall itself, and 227 Battery Headquarters in the Corn Exchange. When 225 Battery moved into the town at the end of the month its headquarters took over the British Legion Hall and later The Liberal Club. The officers were billeted mainly in the Crown and George hotels and the men variously in private houses, public houses, halls, a school and a skittle alley. 226 Battery was stationed in the nearby village of Combe St Nicholas with its headquarters in the Green Dragon Inn.

Shortly after arrival, a warning order was received for the batteries to move in rotation to Lydd camp on the Kent coast for anti-tank gun practice. Although firing was at first put back by two days owing to a lack of ammunition, valuable live practice was gained against moving targets on the range. Hereafter, the training intensified, progressing to tactical exercises by batteries and on to brigade and divisional level to gain experience in inter-arm co-operation. The exercises were spent on the bleak Dorset downs in bitterly cold and wet weather. The training culminated in December with a divisional exercise on Batcombe Down in which the batteries went out with their respective infantry brigades to prepare gun positions as they would in war.

Commanded by Major General E.A. Osborne, the 44th (Home Counties) Division was made up of three infantry brigades, each of

228 Battery, Chard

three Territorial infantry battalions. All were recruited from Surrey, Sussex, Kent and the County of London, as were the supporting artillery, engineers, signals, medical and logistic units. The Regiment was part of the divisional artillery and its batteries would normally be placed under command of the three infantry brigades and with one in reserve.

During the Christmas period only essential work was carried out and on Christmas Day the festivities included a party in the officer's mess and a dance at the Corn Exchange. Christmas dinner and comforts were provided by a fund established by the Mayor of Wimbledon for 'our local anti-tank regiment now stationed somewhere in England'. The local inhabitants also did everything possible for the men's comfort and entertainment and on Boxing Day there were many helpers in the services canteen established in Furnham church room.

The winter turned out to be one of the worst for years and the wet weather was followed in the new year by a cold spell with hard frosts and snow that blocked the narrow country lanes. The vehicles had to be started-up every two or three hours throughout the night to avoid frost damage and the unfortunate driver from being placed on a charge.

The new year also saw the arrival of a new Commanding Officer. On 20 January, Lieutenant-Colonel R.L. Travers, O.B.E., took over from Colonel Imison, who having passed the age for command was released from the Army. The officers gave a farewell dinner for Colonel Imison who was naturally disappointed to be leaving at this juncture. His successor had considerable experience of war on many fronts. In the 1914-18 war he fought in France and Belgium with The Queen's Own Royal West Kent Regiment and was later attached to the West African Frontier Force, taking part in operations to clear the Germans out of East Africa. In 1919-21 he was attached to the 2/9th Gurkha Rifles, fighting rebel tribes on the North West Frontier of India. In 1938 he went to Palestine with the 2nd Royal West Kent, where, the commanding officer having fallen ill, he took over the battalion and conducted operations against the Arab gangs with a success which earned praise in a letter from the Divisional Commander Major-General (later Field Marshal) B.L. Montgomery. He was also mentioned in despatches and awarded the OBE. In 1939, Major Travers was brought home to help train the Militiamen and was promoted at once to command the Royal Artillery Depot at Taunton. Thus it was that an infantry officer of over 25 years experience was given command of the Regiment.

Two other senior appointments at this time were Major G.P. Chapman, D.S.O., M.C., from the Territorial Army Reserve of Officers, as the new Second-in-Command, and Major J.R.C. Christopher, a regular Royal Horse Artillery officer, who took over 226 Battery. The other battery commanders were: Captain T.H. Robinson (225); Captain G.S. Abbott (227); and Captain P.G. Hampton (228).

Due to the huge expansion of the Army, there was a general shortage of officers and to redress the situation a new rank of Warrant Officer Class III was introduced. Classes for potential candidates got underway in January and by the time the Regiment was to go into action half of the anti-gun troops were commanded by the new Troop Sergeant Majors.

Apart from the more recent recruits, the Regiment had arrived in Chard dressed in the old service uniform, but it was now issued with the new battle dress with its loose blouse, baggy trousers, gaiters and webbing equipment. There was some reluctance among the older men to change as the old uniform was seen as a symbol of Territorial service. On the other hand the new battle dress was admittedly more serviceable and comfortable if not smarter.

From the beginning of February the Division concentrated on preparations for its move to join the BEF and the bringing up to scale of vehicles, equipment and personnel took priority. Evidence of this new policy was seen in the Regiment with the arrival of sixteen 2-pounders and a welcome reinforcement of 90 trained men.[2] It was expected that everyone would go within a fortnight and a small advance party left Chard on 4 February for Southampton, but the orders were cancelled and it returned two days later not having embarked. The move to France had been delayed at the last minute as the Division was being held back to go to the aid of Finland against an unprovoked attack launched by Russia.

Training resumed again in earnest with a series of exercises in the continuing bad weather. On 7 February His Majesty King George VI inspected the Division, with the men of the Regiment drawn up in ranks, shoulder to shoulder, lining the road at Crewkerne.

The move to Finland fortunately never took place, for after resisting bravely the Finns were compelled to conclude an armistice with Russia on 13 March. The Division would now be allowed to proceed to France and a warning order was received for the move of the advance party. On the 20th, the party under Second-Lieutenant R.G. Orr finally left Chard and sailed from Southampton.

With the prospect of going into action in the near future, the Regiment was quickly made up to its full war strength of 48 2-pounder guns. Eight guns arrived by train from Woolwich Arsenal and a convoy left for 56th Anti-Tank Regiment in Wantage to collect 25 more. At the same time new Morris gun towers were received to replace the Bedford General Service trucks.

The last days of the month were spent in packing, loading the vehicles and making final preparations for the move, accompanied by inspections from a number of senior officers. During its time in Somerset the Regiment had been toughened up and had trained hard to turn itself into a fighting unit, although it had been continually hampered by a lack of equipment and the appalling weather. The men would undoubtedly miss Chard and its people and many friendships and alliances had been made.

Lieutenant-Colonel Travers addressed all ranks in the afternoon of 31 March to inform them of the orders to move and offered a £5 bounty to the battery that knocked out the first tank and likewise for the first aircraft to be shot down. Two days later the road party with the vehicles and guns left for Southampton under the command of Major

Christopher.[3] The move was made in accordance with the detailed instructions laid down, with the men wearing steel helmets, Bren guns mounted to protect the column against air attack and the vehicles moving at the regulation speed of 15 miles in the hour. After a brief hold-up and a final dash to make up time, the party arrived on schedule and settled down to the business of loading over the next few days.

The main rail party followed on 8 April. The Regiment paraded in Fore Street outside the Corn Exchange at 7.15 a.m. and despite the early hour and supposed secrecy the local people turned out to see them off as they marched to Chard Junction. As one officer recorded: 'It was a quietly thrilling moment. All the months of training and preparation had led up to this, the crowds cheered and cameras clicked and farewell songs were sung. We were off to France.'

NOTES

(1) RHQ and 268 Battery shared the grandstand with the 57th Anti-Tank Regiment and 266 Battery was in the Paddock area. The two other batteries were billeted in Epsom town, 265 in Ebbisham Hall and 267 in Ebbisham Sports Club. The 67th Anti-Tank Regiment formed part of the 12th (Eastern) Infantry Division, a second line Territorial Army division and the duplicate of the 44th Division.

(2) The men arrived in two drafts, 20 posted from the 50th Anti-Tank Training Regiment in Aldershot and 70 from the 52nd Anti-Tank Training Regiment in Bishop Auckland.

(3) The party consisted of 208 officers and men, 122 vehicles, 38 motorcycles and 48 guns. The officers were Major J.R.C. Christopher, Captain V.R.D. Hellaby, Captain N.C. Westwood, Captain R.G. Mayberry, Lieutenant J.C. Elwes and 2/Lieutenant M.A. Edwards.

Chard, Winter 1939-40

November evening and drifting mist
The grey old town in the dwindling light
The billeting officer reading his list
The welcoming doors in the darkening night

And the days that followed; the 'George' and the 'Crown'
And 'The Vicarage' turned to 'The Officers' Mess'
And the Sergeant-Major patrolling the town
And raw young asses in 'Service Dress'

And the rivulets trickling down the street
Past 'RHQ' at the Corn Exchange
And the sound of the Trumpeter blowing 'Retreat'
As the guard formed up for the evening change

The grousing troops in the 'Liberal Club'
The seized up lorries that wouldn't start
The guns to clean – the buttons to rub
And the tramp of boots in the Cattle Mart

Machine gun stripping and rifle drill
The canteen cookies by ladies fond
The convoys of lorries along Cornhill
The pits that we dug in the fields beyond

Two pounder guns on an exercise
On Snowdon Hill – 'Inspection' fuss
The ice bound landscape – 'Mum's' mince pies
Cider – and frost – and the Taunton bus

(Two pounder peashooters! Help us all!
These were expected to settle the Huns!
At thirty metres the Sergeant's bawl
Was far more lethal than all the guns!)

And the nightly sentry pacing his beat
His fingers chilled on his rifle stock
A carpet of snow on the moonlit street
And the distant chime of the striking clock

Christmas in billets. A home made toy
Made as a gift for a boy you met
Was it intended to please the boy
Or impress his sister? (You forget!)

And the kitted ranks on the Springtime day
When we last paraded along the street
A thousand thoughts as we turned away
The gloomy pounding of marching feet

Gunner John Mead

Map 1: The Move to France

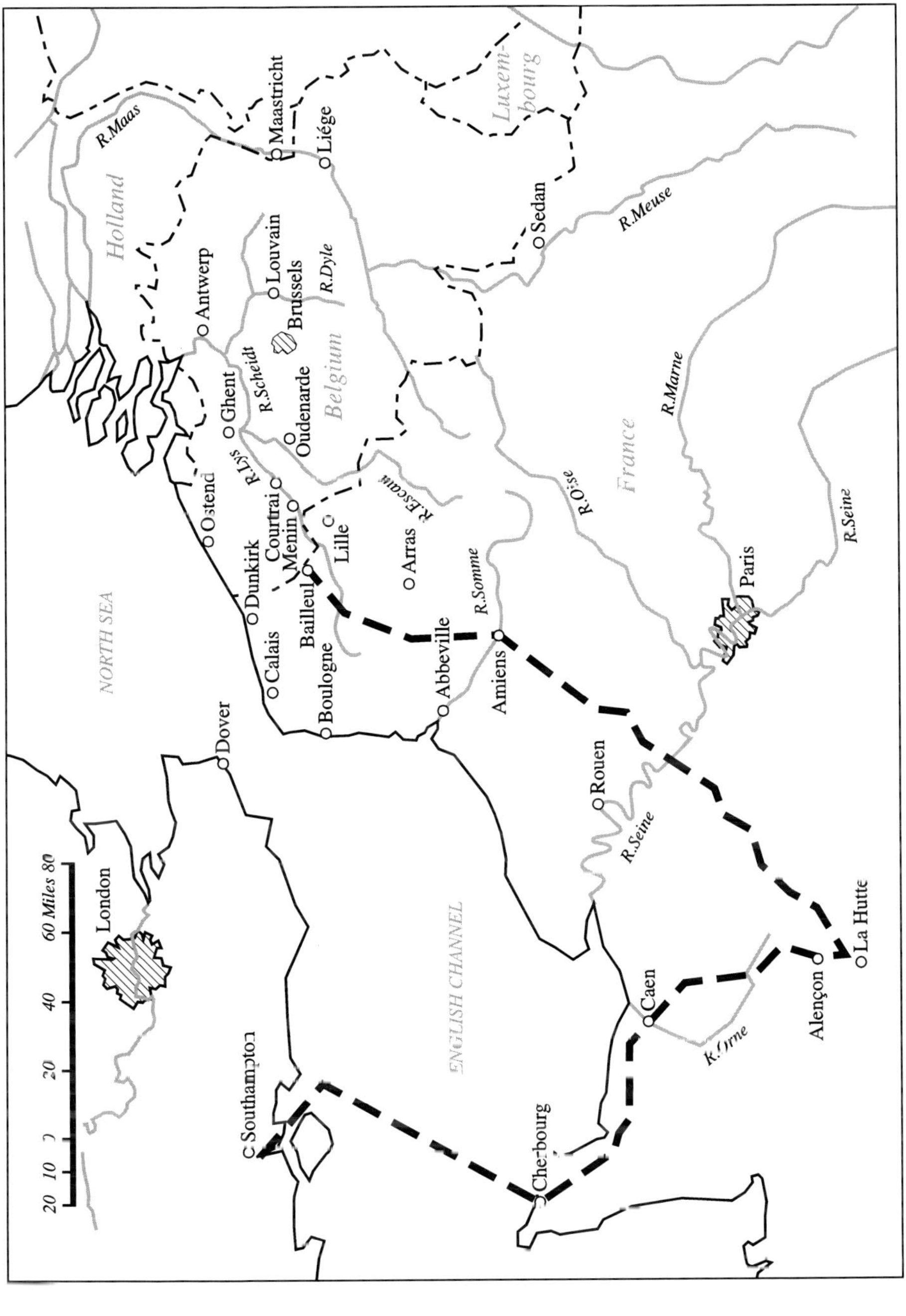

CHAPTER 4

The Move to France

After the Blitzkrieg in Poland, the expected German autumn offensive in the west did not materialise and there followed a six-month lull during which both sides built up their forces, made plans and waited. Though it was not without incident it was a period of minimal aggression referred to as the Phoney War. Along its borders with Germany, the French Army sat behind the Maginot Line. Built in the 1930s, this massive system of fortifications ran from Basle on the Swiss frontier up to Longuy on the frontier with Luxembourg. Neighbouring Belgium clung to a rigid neutrality and would not be party to any joint plan of action, but along the Franco-Belgian frontier there had been dug an almost continuous anti-tank ditch, covered by concrete pill boxes.

The BEF had taken over a sector of the line in the Lille area and set to work to improve the defences. Under command of General Viscount Gort, VC, it originally consisted of the I and II Corps each of two regular divisions. Another regular division was later formed in France and with the arrival of five territorial divisions, including the 44th, a third Corps was completed. The equipment of the force was far from complete, however, especially in the provision of armour. Apart from two battalions equipped with slow moving but heavily armoured infantry tanks, the majority were light tanks and carriers, and the main striking force, 1st Armoured Division, was only due to arrive in May.

Meanwhile the move of the Regiment proceeded apace. Arriving by train from Chard, the main party embarked on the British & Irish cross-channel passenger ship S.S. Louth at Southampton on the afternoon of 8 April. After lying up in the Solent to await darkness and an escort, they crossed at night in a small convoy and reached Cherbourg early the next morning. For many it was their first time overseas and they disembarked in high spirits. A hot, dull day was then spent in a transit camp before entraining in the evening for the journey to the divisional assembly area north of Le Mans.

The train crawled through the night down the Cherbourg Peninsula, stopping at midnight in Caen where the men were given a welcome cup of hot tea and the chance to stretch their legs. They were packed in wooden seated carriages or the '40 Hommes/8 Cheveaux' box cars of First World War fame. At 6 a.m. the following morning they arrived at the small country station of La Hutte, where much to their delight they were met by the regimental transport.

The road party had crossed earlier in the S.S. Fenella, an impressed Isle of Man steamer. After labouring at unloading the vehicles and guns and making ready for the road they set off for the assembly area on 8 April. The somewhat carefree journey was described in a letter home by Second-Lieutenant Mervyn Edwards: 'Then, as always, at the crack of dawn we moved off from the docks. A glorious morning with the flowers and blossom and freshly green trees giving an excellent impression to all, the vast majority of whom had never been in France before. I had the perfectly wizard job of going on ahead of the convoy and fixing up billets for the night. I was surrounded on arrival in the town where we were to stay [Caen] with masses of people who shook me by the hand and owing to my being foolish enough to reveal that I spoke French, I was pestered with all manner of questions before I eventually was able to get down to business in the Town Hall. We stayed in a grand little pub with the most marvellous food all thrown in for 6/- [30p] a night.

'The next day was a titanic struggle against time as I stayed behind to settle up everything and then had to overtake everyone in order to arrive here ahead of the convoy in order to make contact with Gavin [Second-Lieutenant R.G. Orr of the advance party]. However, it was accomplished largely thanks to the marvellous roads which permitted of a colossal average speed and we were able to finish our first stage with flying colours and with a better accident record than almost any previous unit. We picked up the main party in the early hours of the next morning and have spent ever since getting properly connected.'

The Regiment moved into billets in and around the local villages with Regimental Headquarters established at Courgains. In what was to become a familiar pattern, the officers were billeted in private houses and the men in public buildings, farms, barns and outhouses.

Second-Lieutenant Edwards continued: 'We are at the moment resting for a few days in a very pleasant little village, the billets are good and the weather is glorious. There is nothing to really distinguish this village from thousands of others, but the complete absence of men is an extraordinary phenomenon, which has to be seen, if you want to gauge the real effect. Our lives are terribly occupied attending to a steady stream of administrative problems that arise and one of our biggest bogies is of course the censorship of the men's letters, which we all loathe.'

At Courgains, H Section, 2 Company, 44th Divisional Signals under command of Second-Lieutenant G.B. Donald was attached to provide communications for the Regiment. Equipped with No 11 radio sets mounted in 8cwt pick-ups, the section was a group of about two dozen men comprising OWLs (Operators Wireless and Line), Linesmen and Don Rs (Dispatch Riders).

The stay in the assembly area was only to be short as 44th Division was already on the move northwards to take up a position on the frontier in relief of the 51st Highland Division. The latter was going to the Maginot Line on the Saar front to gain valuable experience in contact with the German positions in this sector.

Captain Philip Hampton, commanding 228 Battery, recorded: 'We spent a couple of days at a nearby village and then started our long journey by road through France. We did it by easy stages with halts of varying duration - passing through Amiens and the 1914-18 battlefields. It was a fine sight seeing a complete Anti-Tank Regiment on the road - 124 vehicles and 48 guns. We occupied over 12 miles of road. We never lost our way and never had a serious breakdown, which showed that our previous training had been good. Our journey took us a little under two weeks.'

After staging the first night near Evreux, and crossing the River Seine at Vernon, north-west of Paris, the Regiment reached Fontaine Bonneleau, where Regimental Headquarters was established in a local chateau. A short move was then made to Prouzel, south-west of Amiens, where they remained for five days.

Second-Lieutenant Edwards again: 'Since I last wrote we have been on the move again and are now billeted in a convent of all places. We've managed to make it very comfortable and the old nuns are frightfully kind and helpful. Everyone is in great form and the glorious weather makes life very pleasant indeed. Never having been in a convent before I can't draw comparisons, but its setting is delightful amidst lovely big trees and streams and the aged mother superior readily gave her consent to our holding a service in a quiet corner this morning.'

The final stage was covered on 24 April completing a journey of some 250 miles. Leaving Prouzel, the Regiment passed through Amiens and St Pol, where 227 Battery peeled off north-west to Monchycayeaux to join 133rd Brigade in the reserve training area. The main column moved on to the Bailleul area as Captain Hampton recalled: 'Our last lap took us through country of which we were to know a great deal in the near future. 225 Battery and my own arrived at the village of Le Doulieu at 6 p.m. in pouring rain. While billets were being allotted, the men got down to cleaning their guns and vehicles, all covered in mud. The Brigadier R.A. arrived in the middle to see how things were going, and seemed quite impressed.' Regimental Headquarters and 226 Battery were established in the nearby village of Outtersteene.

The sector of the line taken over by the 44th Division lay between Armentières and Bailleul and it was disposed with 131st Brigade in the right forward sector and 132nd Brigade in the left forward sector. The area was described as a broad, cultivated open plain leading up to and over the frontier and then rising into a line of hills. To the south-east lay Lille and its adjacent industrial complex. The role given to the Division was to continue improving the defensive positions, to assist the French authorities in control of the frontier and to guard the area against an airborne attack. The frontier defences as constructed by the French comprised an almost continuous tank obstacle in the form of a zig-zag ditch covered by a belt of wire and concrete pill-boxes built to mount anti-tank guns and machine guns. After the BEF took over the position the decision was taken to organise the defences in depth with the duplication of successive reserve positions, known collectively as The Gort Line. By the time the offensive opened over 400 pill-boxes had been completed, new wire and obstacles erected and many miles of anti-tank ditch dug.

The Regiment was meanwhile settling down in its new location. The people were mostly friendly, although contact was limited, but the weather turned warm and sunny, with the occasional thunderstorm. Maintenance was carried out on the guns and vehicles, routine training was resumed, morning cross-country runs were instituted and the men set about improving their living conditions. Visits by high ranking officers included Lieutenant General Sir Ronald Adam, Bart., commanding III Corps.

The officers and NCOs were called upon to reconnoitre sites for gun positions and to fix their arcs of fire and this included helping the engineers in the siting of the reserve anti-tank ditch. During this exercise it was discovered that the French-made pill boxes on the forward anti-tank ditch had been built for the French 37mm and the 2-pounders could not be introduced without effectively taking them to pieces. Where gun pits were dug, relics of the previous war were frequently unearthed serving as a reminder that they had returned to the scene close to the old front line.

In the evenings the men walked into Bailleul, or later went by truck to Armentières, to visit the local bars and estaminets and sample the wine and beer, have a sing-song or perhaps try their luck with the mademoiselles. Otherwise they made their own entertainment that included a concert evening. Welcome hot baths were organised at the local pit-heads, which much to the men's amusement were supervised by female attendants.

The period was dogged by rumours of fifth-column activities involving sabotage or covertly supplying information to the enemy. The War Diary records the detention of a suspicious character caught photographing an area adjacent to the guns and one officer recalled that it got to the stage where any concave advertising hoardings were prised open to make sure there were no hidden messages. Usually the rumours were without foundation, but it was psychologically demoralising and it wasted the time of the two liaison officers from the French Army attached to the Regiment. Rumours also abounded about when the offensive would begin as more and more German forces gathered on the frontiers of Belgium, Luxembourg and Holland. The German occupation of Denmark and invasion of Norway earlier in April had heightened expectation that it would soon take place.

A series of different plans were drawn up to meet this eventuality based on the possible lines of defence in Belgium. The one that was adopted was Plan D. This involved a rapid advance of some 75 miles by I and II Corps of the BEF to the River Dyle, east of Brussels, to take up a position between Wavre and Louvain, with the French First Army on its right or southern flank and the Belgian Army on the left northern flank. III Corps with 44th Division in the van was to move forward at the same time and prepare a second line of defence along the River Escaut (or Scheldt in Dutch).

The two weeks the Regiment spent in the frontier area had passed by peacefully enough, but as darkness fell on 9 May the sound of anti-aircraft fire could be heard to the east. Then in the early hours the men were awoken by an air raid warning and donning steel helmets rushed outside or climbed to a vantage point to see the flashes of bombing piercing the darkness in the distance towards Lille and to hear the drone of aircraft overhead. Although they didn't yet know it for certain, but as many suspected, the storm was breaking.

CHAPTER 5

Advance to Contact

The pre-dawn attacks by the Luftwaffe on 10 May heralded the opening moves of the German western campaign. At 4.35 a.m. paratroopers started dropping on key objectives and an hour later its main land forces crossed the frontiers of Luxembourg, Belgium and Holland. The Belgian government asked for help in resisting the invasion and orders were issued by the Allied Supreme Command to put the Dyle Plan into effect.

Official news of the invasion was received by telephone at Regimental Headquarters soon after 8 a.m. together with the order to be prepared to move in six hours. At mid-day Lieutenant-Colonel Travers assembled the senior officers to issue verbal orders for a move to an area south-west of Oudenarde, where 44th Division was to organise the defence of the River Escaut. The Regiment would be one of the first units of the Division to cross the border with the job of providing air cover for the marching infantry along the route, including the protection of vulnerable points like bridges and road junctions. Coupled with its mobility, the Regiment had a high proportion of Bren guns that could be mounted on its vehicles for use against low-flying aircraft to fulfil this role.

The Division was to move on a north-easterly axis with 131st Brigade on the roads astride the River Lys, 132nd Brigade on two routes about three miles to the north, and with 133rd Brigade following in its wake. Regimental Headquarters, 225 and 227 Batteries (the latter brought up from the St Pol training area) were to move with 131st Brigade, while 226 Battery would move independently with 132nd Brigade. The Regiment would have under command some infantry carrier platoons with additional Bren guns.(1)

228 Battery was to be detached in a special role, as Captain Hampton learned having received an urgent message to report to Lieutenant-

Colonel B.T. Godfrey-Faussett, Commander of the 44th Divisional Royal Engineers (CRE), at his headquarters in Estaires. The Battery, as part of a mobile force, was to get to the River Escaut ahead of the Division and guard all the bridges while the engineers prepared them for demolition. The force was to be divided into three groups, each with a troop of anti-tank guns. The final words of the CRE to Captain Hampton were, 'I will see you at Langestraat - you must get there at all costs.'

The batteries spent a busy morning to get everything ready in time for the move and with ammunition issued, set off after lunch for their various starting points. The minutes ticked by until at the appointed hour of 4 p.m., 225 Battery led the Regiment over the frontier at the small village of Romarin, north of Nieppe. The Battery Commander, Captain Tom Robinson, recalled: 'When the balloon finally went up seriously we were first across the line into Belgium. The Belgian frontier guard knew nothing about it, so we pushed the post over and drove on.'

The men were everywhere greeted enthusiastically by the Belgian people, though, lining the roads and cheering them on their way. The main body of the Regiment covered a distance of about 20 miles before arriving in the early hours in the Gheluwe area, north-west of Menin. Here they were joined later by the B Echelon, with the vehicles that carried the ammunition, petrol, rations and other necessities, and which had moved in the rear of the marching troops with the brigade transport. 226 Battery was halted a few miles to the north-west in the Kruiseecke area. For fear that the Germans might be listening in, the move was made in complete radio silence, although this security measure was somewhat compromised by the citizens of Wervicq ringing the church bells in celebration of the arrival of the British troops.

Earlier in the day, Captain Hampton had returned to Le Doulieu to find 228 Battery drawn up in the square in front of the church and ready to move in accordance with his orders. They set off at 2 p.m. and moving via Armentières and Comines crossed over the frontier at Halluin. He recalled: 'We had a magnificent reception all along the

F4354

Advance into Belgium

F4626

Camouflaged 2-pounder and Bren gun team in the front line

route and tea, beer and even money were offered to us whenever we had to pull up. We were approaching Courtrai when I noticed some excitement - people looking up into the sky and pointing. There were aeroplanes up there all right, leaving a faint white exhaust streak behind them - a sight we were to know so well. We carried on into Courtrai where there seemed to be some more excitement with whistles blowing and people going into shelters, etc. As we turned into the main road by the station, I heard a loud whistle and as I turned to look back, I saw the road go up about 100 yards behind me in a mass of brown smoke and flying debris, accompanied by the exploding crash. My driver was looking a bit worried - he had only heard [the explosion]. It was our first taste of being bombed. I said, "it looks as if they are going for the station, the country is our best place so step on it." More explosions were occurring as we raced through the streets, and in about five minutes I pulled up to allow the column to catch up. I was pretty worried as it appeared that my group had caught it. An aerial dogfight was going on overhead and soon a German bomber was spiralling slowly earthwards, until it suddenly dived like a stone, crashed and blew up. A great cloud of dust and smoke hung over the western end of Courtrai. I had never seen anything like this before, and it rather shook me at first. The column soon caught me up and to my surprise I learnt that there were no casualties. Most of my group had had to stop and take cover as the bombs were pretty close. Everyone seemed very cheery and got over their shock, if any, quickly.'

The rest of the journey was uneventful and the column reached Langestraat, on the western slopes that overlook the valley of the River Escaut and about five miles from Oudenarde, in the early evening. There the guns of two troops proceeded to the various bridges spread over a wide front pending the arrival of the main body of the Division.

The Division continued its move the following evening with both brigades now leaving the course of the River Lys around Courtrai to swing eastwards. A tremendous welcome was received as the Regiment passed through the town with 131st Brigade, before it moved on to

Sweveghem, where Regimental Headquarters was established in the Café Bacchus in the early hours of the 12th. Some bombs were dropped close to the columns en route fortunately without causing any damage.

As the Regiment continued its move forward, instead of cheering crowds the roads became congested by civilian refugees flying westwards before the Germans. Second-Lieutenant Edwards wrote: 'We have been given a fair glimpse of this Twentieth Century civilisation during the past few days and have seen one of the most pathetic sights in the world. The endless stream of old men, women and children wearily dragging their ill shod feet over dust laden cobbles and carrying bundles out of all proportion to their size. A spectacle that one will never forget and one that must have been repeated times without number through the ages.'

In the afternoon the Regiment arrived at Caster about a mile behind the Escaut and the vital bridge at Kerkhove. Regimental Headquarters, 225 and 227 Batteries settled into billets in and around the village and linked up with 228 Battery at Langestraat. The latter was to withdraw its guns from the bridges and come back under the command of the Regiment as a mobile reserve. 226 Battery was also nearby in the rear at Anseghem with 132nd Brigade.

The infantry brigades could not be brought forward for the time being as priority was given on the roads to the clearance of the tail of II Corps moving forward to the Dyle. In the meantime reconnaissances got underway to select the battle positions to be occupied on the river and to organise the area for protection against airborne attack. There were numerous reports of landings by parachutists coming in all the time that required investigation and a 'flying' troop of guns was on standby to be dispatched with a mobile column to deal with the threat. However, none of the reports were authenticated.

Tragedy struck on the 13th with the Regiment's first fatality of the war when Bombardier E.F.J. Sellen of 226 Battery was killed in a traffic accident.

Although the first stages of Plan D had been successfully completed, the overall situation was quickly deteriorating and the first signs of danger could be seen in the Sedan area, where the enemy had secured a crossing over the River Meuse. While the Germans were pressing their attacks in the north with vigour, the main effort was concentrated in the centre where the bulk of its armour was allocated to a thrust through the forests of the Ardennes. As this area was thought to be impassable it was manned by reserve French infantry divisions who were stunned by the appearance of German tanks and the incessant attack of dive bombing aircraft. With the French unable to mount an effective counterattack, the German breakout from its bridgehead between Dinant and Sedan got underway on the 14th threatening to destroy the centre of the Allied front and cut its forces in two.

In the north, the Dutch Army capitulated on this day having been similarly unable to respond to the momentum of the German advance and shaken by the bombing of the undefended city of Rotterdam. The Belgian Army had been forced to withdraw towards the Dyle, having lost two unblown bridges over the Meuse and the dominant Fort Eben-Emael designed to protect them to an audacious airborne assault. On the Dyle, the covering armoured regiments of the BEF had withdrawn behind the river, the bridges were destroyed and by evening the first German attacks were underway. The attacks continued along the whole British front throughout the 15th, but were successfully driven off or any penetrations were cleared up by counterattack. During the night the BEF had to withdraw, however, to conform with the French First Army on the right whose front had been broken. The increasing momentum of the enemy attacks also made it clear that a prolonged defence of the Dyle position was impracticable. Accordingly, the next morning a further phased withdrawal was ordered over three successive nights by the French Commander General Billotte, first to the River Senne (a line running through Brussels) then to the River Dendre (some ten miles behind Brussels) and finally to the Escaut (a further twenty miles to the rear).

In order to be ready to cover this withdrawal, moves were carried out to bring the troops of 44th Division forward to the line of the Escaut into locations near their battle positions to start work on the defences and take over guards on the bridges. The sector covered a five mile frontage of the river running in a valley from the outskirts of Eyne north of Oudenarde to the small hamlet of Eeuwhoek. From across the river the position was overlooked by sharply rising wooded country, but on the west or British side the slope rose gently with the crest of the ridge about one mile back. The river itself was bordered by low lying meadow land, intersected by tree-lined boundaries and with plenty of copses. The main road ran parallel with the river about 500 yards from the river bank until it crossed the plain between the village of Petegem and Oudenarde. To the rear of the road ran the main Brussels railway. The sector was on the extreme left or northern flank of the British line at the junction with the Belgians and where the Germans could be expected to exert pressure. To the south the line extended to Maulde on the French frontier with a further six divisions of the BEF deployed along it.

With the move forward, the battery commanders reconnoitred their areas to select gun positions, not just in the divisional sector but also on both flanks. Close attention was given in siting the guns to cover the main bridges and roads. On the 15th Captain R.E.A. Foulger handed over the adjutancy to Captain Robinson and took over 225 Battery. The key appointments (officers and warrant officers) in the Regiment at this time are shown in Appendix D.

At 4 a.m. on the 17th emergency instructions were received at Regimental Headquarters to place anti-tank guns on all bridges. This action was prompted by news coming in of the German breakthrough in the south, where the panzers were driving hard for the coast through the shattered French divisions. Moving by night and day, the leading armoured units had reached Le Cateau on this morning and now posed a serious threat to the rear of the BEF.(2) 225 Battery, later relieved by 228, was despatched for this task and there they witnessed the start of the arrival of the units falling back from the Dyle.(3) Captain Hampton observed: 'By 8 a.m. the guns were all in position over a 10 mile front again. My advanced headquarters were at Bossuyt on the banks of the river seven miles south of Oudenarde. It was a lovely day and everything was quiet. Before long we began to see signs of the retreat: first odd vehicles, then more and more until finally one long stream. I talked to some of them - yes, they had been in action, and the Germans were tough. Many tanks and thousands of men. The rearguard was having a bad time trying to hold the enemy back until new positions were taken up. They had been machine gunned from the air too.'

In addition to I and II Corps, 10 Belgian Division was also coming through to occupy the sector on the left or north of 44th Division. Captain Gerry Mayberry of 225 Battery recalled: 'I remember watching Belgian horse-drawn artillery coming back through us with their fellows falling asleep on their horses. All I could think of was this must be something like the battle of Waterloo and I shall never see the like of it again.'

Ahead of and intermingled with the troops were the mass of refugees who poured over the bridges and through the town of Oudenarde, whose inhabitants were ordered to evacuate their homes and join the flight westwards.

While 228 was guarding the bridges this day, the three other batteries moved forward to their battle positions. Regimental Headquarters was established in the rear on a farm near Anseghem and close to 44th Divisional Headquarters at Kruisweg. The next morning the anti-tank fire plan was formulated following a co-ordination reconnaissance on the ground by the CRA(4), Brigadier E.P.H. Pease Watkin, with Lieutenant-Colonel Travers, Captain Robinson and representatives from the field regiments.

The Division was disposed with two brigades forward and one in reserve. On the left was 132nd Brigade with one battalion in Oudenarde and one further north, while depth was given by the third battalion at Eekhout. On the right was 131st Brigade also with two battalions forward on the river and one in reserve. The four forward battalions each held a frontage of 2,500-3,000 yards, but between the two brigades there was a gap, responsibility for which was never properly co-ordinated. 133rd Brigade was on the reserve line north of Steenbrugge.

The artillery was organised into two groups, each with two field regiments to cover one of the forward brigades. The Regiment, less two batteries, co-ordinated the anti-tank dispositions with the field regiments within their zones with 225 Battery deployed on the left and 227 on the right. 226 Battery was under command of 131st Brigade, less E Troop with 132nd Brigade. 228 Battery would take up positions on the reserve line when relieved of responsibility for the bridges.

The men worked hard all day digging gun pits and strengthening them with earth, sandbags and timber. During all this period the weather was hot and sunny and thick dust lay everywhere. The long spell of dry weather combined with the closing of the sluice gates farther south led to a drop in the level of the river by 5-6 feet making it a much less formidable obstacle. To deny the enemy any footholds across the river, any barges were towed to the near bank and sunk, while charges were placed on all the road and railway bridges and firing parties stood by to execute the demolition at short notice.

On the morning of the 19th, the increase in enemy air activity escalated into bombing raids on the bridges and town of Oudenarde. Several direct hits were scored on the large road bridge at Eyne causing a number of casualties. In the town itself many houses were struck and set on fire, and on the Egypten bridge an ammunition truck belonging to L Troop was caught and destroyed and another was seriously damaged with two men slightly wounded. The raid was witnessed by I Troop, which had its headquarters and Number One gun covering the bridge. Driver D. Younghusband showed considerable coolness in helping the L Troop detachment to get its gun out of a dangerous position by reversing his truck over the bombed bridge and bringing both the gun and crew to I Troop Headquarters.

In the early evening the various bridges were successfully demolished, leaving just one intact at Oudenarde and where the rearguard covering the withdrawal of the troops from the Dyle was anxiously awaited. As the bridges were blown the guns of I Troop returned to 227 Battery in the Caster area and went into previously selected positions. 228 Battery handed over to II Corps troops and withdrew to Jammelshoek about four miles back from the river.(5) At about 8 p.m. the light tanks and carriers of the divisional cavalry forming the rearguard rattled over the last bridge and it was finally blown just before midnight.

The powerful demolitions that shook the night together with the arrival of several shells that fell near the town conveyed to everyone that the waiting was over and that action was imminent. With its characteristic brevity the War Diary closed for the night with the entry: 'Large enemy attack now expected. Our preparations made.'

NOTES

(1) Each infantry battalion had a platoon of ten carriers - lightly armoured tracked vehicles, each with a driver and a crew of three with a Bren gun. The carrier platoons of the 1/5th and 1/6th Queen's were under command of the main body of the Regiment and the platoon of the 5th Royal West Kent under 226 Battery.

(2) Scene of a famous delaying action in 1914 fought by the British II Corps, and notably the field artillery, against the greater part of the First German Army.

(3) 227 Battery was also ordered to send one troop (I) to Oudenarde to guard bridgeheads and relieve one troop of 226 Battery.

(4) Commander Royal Artillery: the brigadier who commands the artillery of a division and advises the divisional commander on artillery matters.

(5) With the arrival of 4th Division of II Corps from the Dyle, which moved in on the right of the 44th, the defence of the Kerkhove bridge was taken over by the 1st East Surreys. Further to the right was the Regiment's former sister Territorial battalion 1/6th East Surreys.

Map 2: Oudenarde and the Escaut

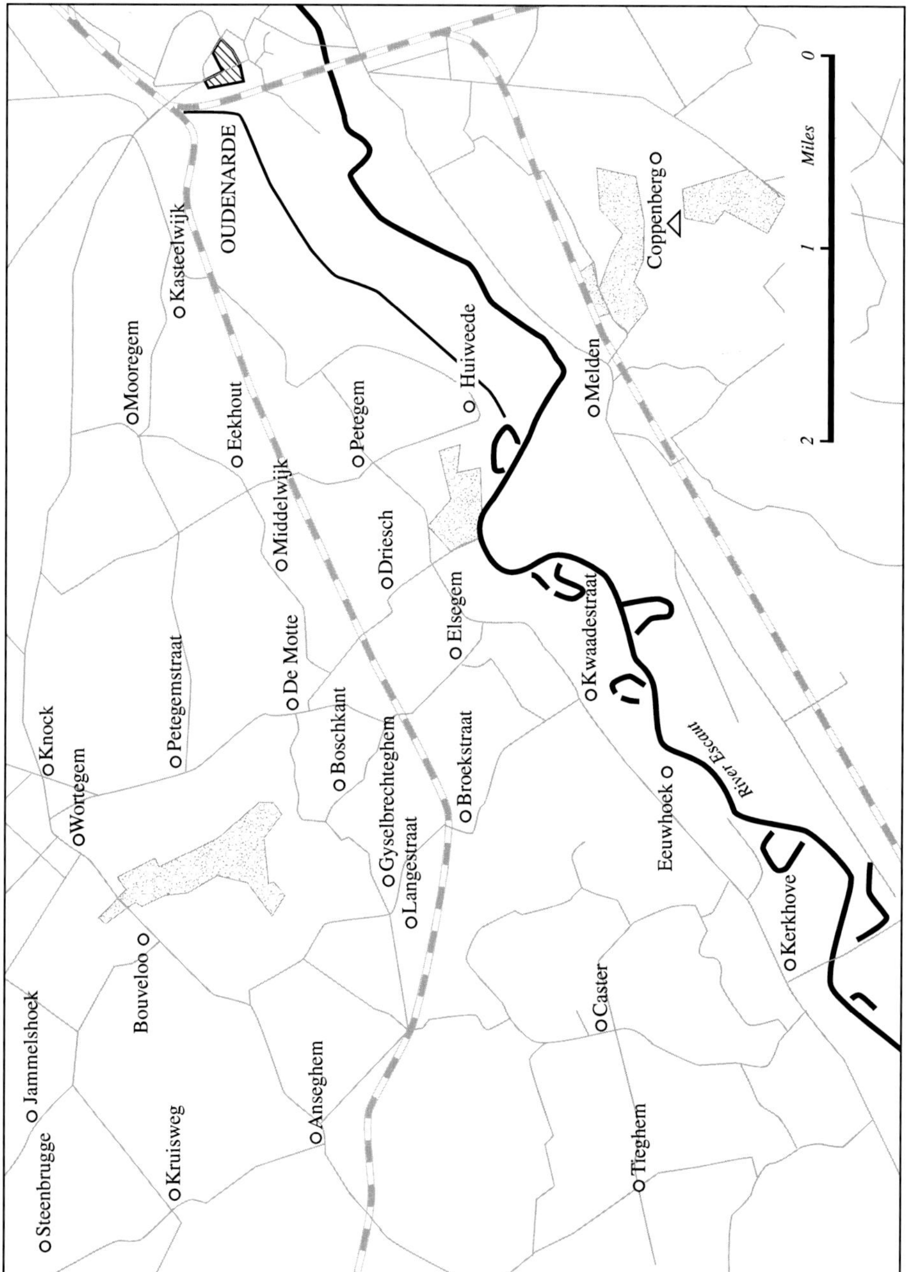

CHAPTER 6

Battle on the Escaut

'Stand to' on Monday 20 May was at 3.30 a.m., before daybreak and the onset of another hot sunny day. During the morning German patrols approached to reconnoitre the river, but it was not until just before midday that the first troops arrived to take up positions on the opposite bank. They were observed cycling down the wooded hill into Melden and were at first thought to be refugees, but were in fact the forward bicycle companies of the 30th Infantry Division.

Reports of their arrival were passed back to the field gunners who greeted them with a bombardment. Harassing fire was then continued throughout the afternoon on any observed troop concentrations and to hinder attempts to bring forward bridging materials.

The 30th Division planned to make its attack with the 6th and 46th Infantry Regiments(1), each with two battalions up front. The 6th Regiment was to cross the river in front of the Belgians on the northern flank around Zingem, while the Oudenarde sector was allocated to the 46th Regiment.

The start of the battle from the British perspective is described in *Destination Dunkirk*: 'The Germans opened their attack on the 44th Division by making a crossing against the right battalion of the right brigade, the 1/6th Queen's of the 131st. This was at 3.30 p.m. and it was accompanied by the widespread fall of shells and mortar bombs and by machine gun fire on many points along the 2,600 yards held by this battalion astride the village of Elsegem. The Queen's retaliated vigorously under the close supervision of Brigadier Utterson-Kelso... Having seen the Germans thrown back at two points by bold use of carriers, he summoned a company of his reserve, the 1/5th Queen's, while the 1/6th's reserve company launched a counterattack against a larger intrusion of Germans.'

The guns of the Regiment were also on the receiving end of the enemy shelling as Gunner Joe Courtney of G Troop, 227 Battery, recalled: 'Our first initiation to gun fire came when a salvo of heavy shells exploded around our position killing the popular Sergeant Reaney and wounding another.[2] The gun fire lifted and a heavy bombardment fell among the field artillery just behind us. At the same time mortar bombs and machine gun fire were steadily increasing against our infantry, and we were getting our fair share as well. We received the order to 'take post' in anticipation of an armoured attack...'

Having failed to gain a footing on the 1/6th Queen's front, the Germans transferred their pressure to that of the 2nd Buffs on the left of the 131st Brigade front. Here a large right-angled bend in the river ran round the Buffs right flank, making it exposed to two directions and as dusk was falling the II Battalion of 46th Regiment was able to get across into the woodland south of Petegem and the hamlet of Huiweede. Defensive fire was put down by all the available field guns and around midnight a counterattack using carriers was made by way of the sunken road to Huiweede, but could not be maintained. A second counterattack was also brought to a standstill as dawn was breaking on the 21st.

With their first day's objective of securing small bridgeheads over the Escaut achieved, the Germans terminated their main attacks for the time being while reinforcements were brought up. The northern crossing at Zingem was abandoned and all resources were allocated to planning a decisive breakthrough south of Oudenarde later on in the day, with two battalions of the 26th Regiment to be thrust in on the right of the 46th.

In the bridgehead fighting continued with parties of German troops infiltrating into the outskirts of and beyond Petegem under the cover of an early morning mist. One German section penetrated as far as Eekhout in the 132nd Brigade sector, whose defenders stood firm, but a counterattack launched towards Petegem could get no further than the railway line about a quarter of a mile from it. 1/5th Queen's, also

The bridge at Eyne after being bombed by the Luftwaffe

Wrecked barges on the River Escaut at Oudenarde

committed to check the enemy's advance, sent its carriers into the village from the west to find it a shambles of burning houses and corpses.

The dangerous situation in the Petegem area led to many gun detachments in 226 Battery fighting in trenches as infantry and it was feared that some of the forward guns deployed to bring fire on the main road had been overrun or destroyed and the detachments taken prisoner. As a precaution the ammunition trucks in the battery area were withdrawn to the rear near Regimental Headquarters. Further casualties were caused in the batteries by the heavy and accurate shelling of the German guns. The fire was directed by an enemy spotter plane, that flew unmolested overhead for most of the day registering targets, and from observers on the high ground of the Coppenberg and Mont de Enclus. Gun pits were cratered, the ground was ploughed up and landmarks swallowed up in clouds of dust. Captain Foulger and Lieutenant E.R. Hutton in 225 Battery had narrow escapes when the roof of their farm billet fell in during a bombardment.

In the afternoon, the Germans resumed their attack, supported by field guns and heavy corps artillery. On the approach to the river, the battalions were struck in return by well directed British artillery fire, but once across they pushed on quickly to the railway and in stubborn house to house fighting finally overwhelmed any resistance in Petegem. Under the weight of a continued British bombardment and machine gun fire that swept the brow of the railway embankment south of Eekhout they then became disorganised and heavy casualties were sustained. As a result the attack was called off and the troops ordered to concentrate on holding the positions gained for the night. With Oudenarde still held firmly by the 4th Royal West Kent, the III Battalion of the 26th Regiment was also brought forward and formed a screen south of Kasteelwijk.

Farther south the I Battalion of 46th Regiment crossed the river and battled on towards the railway line against tough resistance from the 1/6th Queen's. With German troops in the rear of the battalion positions and with no more reserves available to restore the situation, the bulk of 131st Brigade started to withdraw to the high ground between Anseghem and Knock. The final retirement is described in *Destination Dunkirk*: 'As night was falling a remnant of the Queen's managed to fight their way back from their long held and widely extended defences, having lost over 400 of their comrades killed, wounded or captured, and the Buffs did likewise from their chateau near the river... The Germans peppered the rearguards hard but did little to waylay the ragged groups that trudged back through the darkness with grim determination to survive.'

As the battle died down the 44th Division front was held in the centre by the 2nd Royal Sussex (sent forward in the morning) on the railway between Broekstraat and Middelwijk and with some of the 1/5th Queen's on their left. The 132nd Brigade formed a flank with the 1st and 4th Royal West Kent, together with a company of the Buffs, also about the railway between Eckhout and Oudenarde and with the 5th Royal West Kent still holding its original positions north of the town. On the right the withdrawal of the two Queen's battalions meant that the left hand battalions of 4th Division had to face left to cover the new open flank. From the German perspective, 30th Division had five battalions over the river and a bridgehead over a mile deep and nearly two miles wide.

During the afternoon the two remaining battalions of 133rd Brigade had also been brought up to occupy a more forward reserve line, with the 4th Royal Sussex dug in on the right about Anseghem and the 5th Royal Sussex on the left about Knock. In support, 228 Battery was ordered to form an anti-tank barrier in the Petegemstraat area to cover the left flank. Captain Hampton detailed the four guns of K Troop under Second-Lieutenant G. Douglas and two more from Second-Lieutenant L.W. Goodman's L Troop - the whole to be under command of Captain V.R.D. Hellaby. Captain Hampton explained: 'I selected these two as I considered them to be the best of my officers and I felt that things might get nasty there. I also decided to take my other six guns up forward in case they were needed... That evening we moved up the guns. Gordon [Douglas] went straight to his area while Victor [Hellaby] and I with the remainder went more to the front and settled down in a deserted farm. Shelling started at once and a 25 pounder some 50 yards away received a direct hit. There was a lot of noise going on and infantry coming back said the shelling was awful. They had obviously had a tough time and did not like it.'

As night fell the men of the battery looked out on a landscape of destruction illuminated by the glow of burning buildings and the intermittent flashes of field guns. Captain Hampton was later ordered to take back the six guns not detailed for the anti-tank barrier and hide them near the Divisional Headquarters at Huttegem. Just before leaving, he told Captain Hellaby that he would get back as soon as he could and rejoin him, but the two were not destined to meet again until after the war. The barrier itself was further strengthened by four guns of I Troop from 227 Battery.

Lieutenant-Colonel Travers issued a special operation order to all batteries that night stating that there would be no withdrawal and that the Regiment would fight to the 'LAST man and the LAST round' in its present positions.(3) The order was issued no doubt as a result of a message sent by the CRA to all artillery regiments in 44th Division that no guns were to be withdrawn. It originated from a request to General Osborne to withdraw a troop per battery in one of the field regiments, presumably as a precaution against the guns being overrun. Apparently certain that they were safe, General Osborne ordered them to remain in position and fight it out.

Another somewhat contradictory message was sent by the Commander III Corps Artillery giving Passchendaele as the rendezvous in the event of a withdrawal. As *Destination Dunkirk* explained: 'This was somehow converted in transmission to regiments to an order to fire ammunition and destroy guns. It resulted, through differences in inclination and interpretation, in the destruction of half the guns of the 58th Field and in the withdrawal to Passchendaele of all except two bogged ones of the 65th Field, who were supporting the 132nd Brigade.

The 44th Division were in no position to afford such wanton loss.' The artillery situation was weakened further with the withdrawal of the 139th Army Field Regiment supporting 131st Brigade to cover the bridges over the River Lys.

The combination of the deployment of the Regiment's guns across the whole divisional front and the fluid nature of the fighting made it difficult to draw a completely accurate picture of the situation. In the main, the battery locations conformed to the dispositions on the battlefield: in the centre the guns of 226 Battery still in action were behind the railway line; on the left the forward guns of 225 Battery and E Troop of 226 were engaged in the fight north of Petegem; and on the right the guns of 227 Battery were on the Caster ridge, apart from the troop with 228 Battery forming the anti-tank barrier at Petegemstraat. The individual gun detachments generally had little or no idea, however, of what was happening elsewhere and were afflicted by a lack of sleep and the effects of the constant shelling and mortaring. Although the guns were sited where possible to give mutual support, they were often quite isolated and had no way of communicating with one another. The sometimes conflicting and alarmist reports given by stragglers coming through the gun positions also did nothing to improve the morale of those waiting for the enemy's attack.

Despite the 'stand and fight' exhortations, it was the consensus of all three corps commanders that the Escaut line could not be held longer than the following night and Lord Gort undertook to obtain the consent of his allies for a withdrawal. It was eventually agreed that the British Army would pull back to their old and much better developed positions on the French frontier between Halluin and Maulde and the Belgian Army would conform by withdrawing to the River Lys. The 44th Division was to occupy a sector on the Lys between Harlebeke and Menin before being relieved by the Belgians.

The morning of Wednesday 22 May was ominously quiet to begin with, but it was not long before the whole line was subjected to shelling and probing attacks developed in the direction of Eekhout and increasingly towards Kasteelwijk. The situation was checked temporarily by the bold use of carriers, travelling at high speed and firing bursts of light machine gun fire, penetrating the enemy's positions.

At 10 a.m. Captain G.S. Abbott, commanding 227 Battery, was ordered to withdraw the four forward guns in the Caster area behind the railway line to the Anseghem - Knock area. Later the remainder of the Battery followed suit and 226 Battery went into reserve. Gunner Joe Courtney summed up the movement as follows: 'Orders were issued to get some of the guns out as best we could. This we did with a little help from the Jerry mortars.'

One of the guns on the right of the 227 position could not be located. It had in fact been overrun as Gunner Albert Tizzard, a member of the detachment, related: 'We were told to hold our position until ordered to withdraw, but were left where we were and no orders were received to evacuate the position. Having heard the sound of vehicles on the move, we began to fear that the enemy had broken through. Soon after we then heard the sound of voices and marching feet. I volunteered to investigate and when I got to the road, I saw a company of Germans... I raced back to the gun team and gave them our situation. We removed the firing pin from our gun and decided to try and get away, but were spotted by the enemy who quickly surrounded us and made escape impossible. We were then disarmed and all five of us marched down to a farm in the village, where we were shut in a shed with straw on the floor and guards outside.'

Driver Bill Hinton's detachment of D Troop was more fortunate in being able to pull out in the nick of time: 'Our Sergeant gave us orders to stand by our Bren gun, until our driver got the lorry loaded and started with our 2-pounder hooked up. I was Number One on the Bren gun and my Number Two was Ernie Rogers. At the last minute, Ernie and myself were to get mounted, but the lorry would not start. Our driver, Chalkie Walker, was doing his best to get it going, but by then the Germans were only a matter of two or three hundred yards away... We all thought 'this is it', then the truck burst into life and we took off as though we were at Le Mans!'

The main German onslaught got underway again in the afternoon after the re-organisation of the units of 30th Division and the further strengthening of its artillery with three heavy batteries. Under the cover of a massive bombardment, the three battalions of the 46th Regiment were launched across the railway line between Broekstraat and Middelwijk, while the 26th Regiment with two battalions forward thrust once again toward Eekhout and Kasteelwijk. To the south the German 19th Infantry Division launched a full scale assault across the river against Kerkhove and into the flank of the left hand battalion of the British 4th Division.

Although there were some penetrations, the Germans were unable to get across the railway line in numbers on the 132nd Brigade front and the position remained intact until the evening. The resolute defence of Eekhout particularly disrupted the enemy's plans and it was in this area that Second-Lieutenant Mervyn Edwards won an immediate Military Cross on the recommendation of General Osborne. One of the guns of E Troop had been under heavy shell fire for three quarters of an hour when, as the citation records: 'Second-Lieutenant Edwards, with great difficulty, reached his gun, where he instilled courage and calmness into the whole of the detachment. He was ordered to withdraw his gun, and by his skilful handling was able to get it hooked on to his truck and out of action without any casualties. Undoubtedly the lives of his detachment were saved by his cool-headedness and complete disregard of his own safety in a most difficult situation.'

In the centre of the line the Germans made better progress against 133rd Brigade. Working round the separate defence localities of the 2nd Royal Sussex, the most dangerous penetration was made on the left flank to bring pressure on the 5th Royal Sussex on the high ground in front of Knock and the covering anti-tank barrier at Petegemstraat. Under the weight of continued attacks, the gun detachments forming the barrier desperately resisted the German advance until lack of ammunition and wounds forced them to withdraw or surrender. The experience of a K Troop section is recorded in the citation for the Military Cross awarded to its officer Second-Lieutenant Douglas: 'Heavy dive-bombing destroyed one of the guns of the section, killing the detachment (less one man). Lieutenant Douglas continued for two hours to hold his position with the remaining gun and two Bren guns. It was attacked three times by the enemy infantry. The first two attacks were broken up by his determined resistance. In the third heavy attack his position was entirely surrounded, but for two hours he held on until almost every round of small arms ammunition was expended and the enemy infantry had closed in. He then fired off all the remaining anti-tank shells and (having no lanyard) showed great coolness in destroying his own gun by putting a round down the muzzle and firing the gun by kicking the emergency firing lever; in doing so he was wounded in the face and chest.'

Throughout the whole action Second-Lieutenant Douglas was gallantly supported by Lance Bombardier C. W. Dunn who was awarded a Military Medal. The two men were taken prisoner, along with Captain Hellaby, who was also wounded, Sergeant H. Bartlett and others. Of the six anti-tank guns from 228 Battery forming the barrier, three were lost and three were brought back by Second-Lieutenant Goodman, although the latter did not rejoin the Regiment until the following morning.

Sergeant W. Baker, who was a Number One of an I Troop gun detachment at Petegemstraat, was also put forward for a Mention in Despatches. The citation read: 'In the face of a determined advance by enemy infantry [this NCO] remained himself and kept his whole detachment at their gun position. In spite of very heavy shelling, which had been continuing for three days, and enemy small arms fire, he brought all available small arms fire to bear and finally used his 2-pounder anti-tank gun with considerable effect. The whole detachment is missing, but when last seen they were still keeping up a furious fire until eventually overrun.'(4)

The order to withdraw to the River Lys reached the units of 44th

Division in the late afternoon and with the move to take place at nightfall, they faced the difficult task of breaking contact with the enemy in the dark. The constant shelling also made it difficult to maintain communications with signal lines broken everywhere. The 1st East Riding Yeomanry, sent forward to cover the withdrawal, would provided a protective screen of light tanks and carriers along the line from Anseghem through Knock to Waalem. Its orders were to remain in position until 2 a.m. the following morning when all the troops should have passed through. 228 Battery was detailed to assist the yeomanry in its role by placing the six reserve guns round the Divisional Headquarters at Huttegem. In view of the uncertainty of the situation, its B Echelon was sent back to Courtrai straight away.

In the 133rd Brigade area, the forward companies of the 2nd Royal Sussex on the railway line were the first to pull back. Following up, the enemy reached the Bouveloo ridge on the left flank of the brigade front and forced the 5th Royal Sussex to retire to new positions in the houses and gardens of Knock and Wortegem. The front of the 4th Royal Sussex forward of Anseghem was denied to the enemy, however, until the withdrawal took place around 10 p.m.

The Regimental War Diary stated that the batteries were not ordered to withdraw until after 11 p.m. and added: 'Operation carried out with great difficulty, but in fairly good order. Completed before midnight.' Regimental Headquarters pulled out of its farm near Anseghem, now ablaze, with shells falling around the position and with Verey lights on the ridge in front marking the German advance. Gunner Frank Grove, sent as a dispatch rider with a message to one of the batteries, recalled: 'There was a great deal of movement during the night... with infantry going through our lines. After this, Bren gun carriers were going like the clappers to our rear. Then we boarded trucks going in the same direction.'

The bulk of the Regiment withdrew on the southern route to Courtrai via Kruisweg, Hierwieg, Vichte and Steenbrugge, although everyone was by this time too tired perhaps to notice. Captain Hampton, with the 228

Battery rearguard, wrote: 'There was no news of Victor [Hellaby] and company so I could only hope they were getting out all right. At 12.45 a.m. on 23 May, we pushed off. Some infantry were marching back, but apart from them we were about the last. Odd fires were burning in the distance as we began the first of our many withdrawals.' On arrival, the Regiment was to place its guns on the bridgeheads over the River Lys.

225 Battery, together with some gun detachments from 226, withdrew on the northern route via Waereghem, Deerlyck and Harlebeke. The story is told in *Destination Dunkirk*: 'The Royal West Kent battalions had the furthest to come. They withdrew from Oudenarde at dusk, and with the stout protection from two flankguard companies successfully made their escape round the northern side of the bulge the Germans had made into the divisional line. They had then to march 15 miles to the River Lys, often bumping into each other in the state of semi-consciousness into which they fell on relaxation of the strain of three days' close contact with the enemy. The two rearguard companies had the bridge over the Lys blown up by a Belgian just ahead of them and had to continue for a further three miles into Courtrai. Ten days previously they had marched proudly through its streets and been cheered by the people. Now the streets were deserted, pock-marked, littered with debris, and strewn with telephone wires, and the soldiers were grimy, sagging and grey; but still proud…'

Driver Jack Boswell of 225 Battery provided a first-hand account: 'One evening towards dusk the West Kents came streaming through our position and told us that the Germans had crossed the river at two points and were right behind, so we limbered up the gun and tagged along. We halted on the main road and one of their officers told us to make for Courtrai as quickly as possible. Speed was out of the question, the road was packed with Belgian troops most of them without weapons and they seemed to have lost interest in the proceedings. Owing to the numbers on the road I could only drive in low gear and I was wondering if the petrol would last out. After a while I was flagged down by a group of West Kents who asked me if I would take two of their wounded comrades on board. Our Number One agreed so I let down the tailboard in order to lay one man down who had been wounded in the stomach, the other man was hit in the thigh and we put him on the seat where my sergeant usually sat next to me. The remainder of the group clambered on to the tailboard of the truck and also on the shield and trail of the gun. We set off once more, this time we were on our own and after a while the truck ground to a halt as we had run out of fuel. After checking with a dipstick I could see that there was still three gallons in the tank, I had forgotten to switch on the emergency tap. Then I had the problem of getting the petrol from the tank up to the autovac and down to the carburettor. Everybody was getting anxious because we were alone in the darkness and the Jerries were right behind us. We carried on until we reached Courtrai where we deposited the wounded in the local hospital. The gun was got into action on one of the bridges across the river and some of the crew went on the scrounge for food. Normal rations were not available so we had to live on what we could find. The town was in a mess having been bombed by the Luftwaffe on the day before.'

Some of the individual gun teams that had not received the order to cover the bridgeheads on the Lys found themselves being pulled out of the columns to do so as they crossed the river in the early hours. At least one team was on the wrong side of the river as a bridge was blown forcing them to find another crossing. The roads were also very congested and Joe Courtney recalled that their bridge was blocked by a swarm of refugees who had to be pushed aside for the guns to get through.

The Regiment reassembled behind the Lys in the early hours of 23 May and set about collecting those guns and vehicles that had become detached in the night. By morning the bridgeheads on the river from Harlebeke to Courtrai were covered by 226 Battery and from Courtrai to Menin by a composite battery of 225 and 227 guns. Regimental Headquarters was established at Oudenmolen, near Moorseele to the north of Menin, and to where 228 Battery withdrew its guns and was

F4484

Exhausted Belgian horse-drawn artillery during the withdrawal

French prisoners of war taking a brief rest in Oudenarde town square

placed 'on wheels' in reserve. All the bridges were demolished by the engineers after the last troops had crossed, apart from two large ones in Courtrai. The surviving southernmost bridge was then fired but it remained in situ and additional charges had to be inserted. The work took several hours and gave the covering gun detachment and infantry party an anxious wait as the enemy were expected to arrive at any time. The bridge was blown again later in the morning and as a result of the demolition it vanished completely.

From the British perspective, the withdrawal from the River Escaut had been successfully carried out. The Division had drawn clear away from the enemy and there had been little interference en route. On arrival in the Courtrai area, it was also able to get more rest than expected as it was found that the sector the Division had been ordered to hold, was already occupied by Belgian troops in accordance with their earlier undertaking.

The Regiment meanwhile took stock of its situation. In addition to the known casualties, several detachments were missing and there had been a considerable loss of guns, vehicles and equipment. A situation report produced in the morning gave the number of guns in possession subject to confirmation as 30, representing a loss of nearly 40 percent.

The policy on the Escaut position had been to prevent the enemy crossing the anti-tank obstacle, i.e. the river, and therefore it was felt acceptable that a certain proportion of the 2-pounders could be placed well forward. Although it placed them in danger, it was consistent with pre-war thought on the employment of anti-tank guns that a large proportion of them stood a good chance of being overrun by enemy armoured fighting vehicles and/or destroyed by the enemy artillery. The shelling and mortaring had certainly been heavy, but no German tanks were deployed. The Regiment had therefore been unable to fulfil its primary function and the losses were caused primarily by the gun positions being overrun by infantry. Captain Hampton's comment on rejoining the Regiment at Oudenmolen summed up its experiences: 'I found the Commanding Officer a little later and heard the awful news that we had lost 17 guns without seeing a tank - all overrun by Germans.' Moreover, there had been a positive resolve to stay on the Escaut, but as things got progressively worse and the order to withdraw was given there was the start of a feeling that things were not going quite to plan.

Back on the Escaut, the German 30th Division had been planning for a continuation of the attack, but an armed reconnaissance at first light on the 23rd revealed that the British had gone. Pursuit groups on bicycles, pushing forward along the lines of attack, everywhere reported evidence of the withdrawal and by the evening of the same day, the vanguard of the division was standing on the east bank of the Lys.

NOTES

(1) A German Regiment was similar in composition to a British Infantry Brigade, each with three infantry battalions, numbered I, II and III, i.e. II Battalion, 46th Regiment.

(2) Sergeant Douglas Reaney who is buried in Caster churchyard.

(3) See Appendix F for the full text of the order.

(4) Sergeant Baker was made a prisoner of war.

During the battle, a party of men of the Regiment were approached by an officer of the 1/8th Middlesex Regiment (a machine gun battalion attached to 44th Division) and he asked if any of the gunners knew how to use the Vickers .303 medium machine gun. The men, many of whom were former 5th East Surreys, were able to oblige and carried out a number of shoots on enemy targets. This event, at first thought to be apocryphal has since been confirmed as accurate.

Map 3: The Canal Line

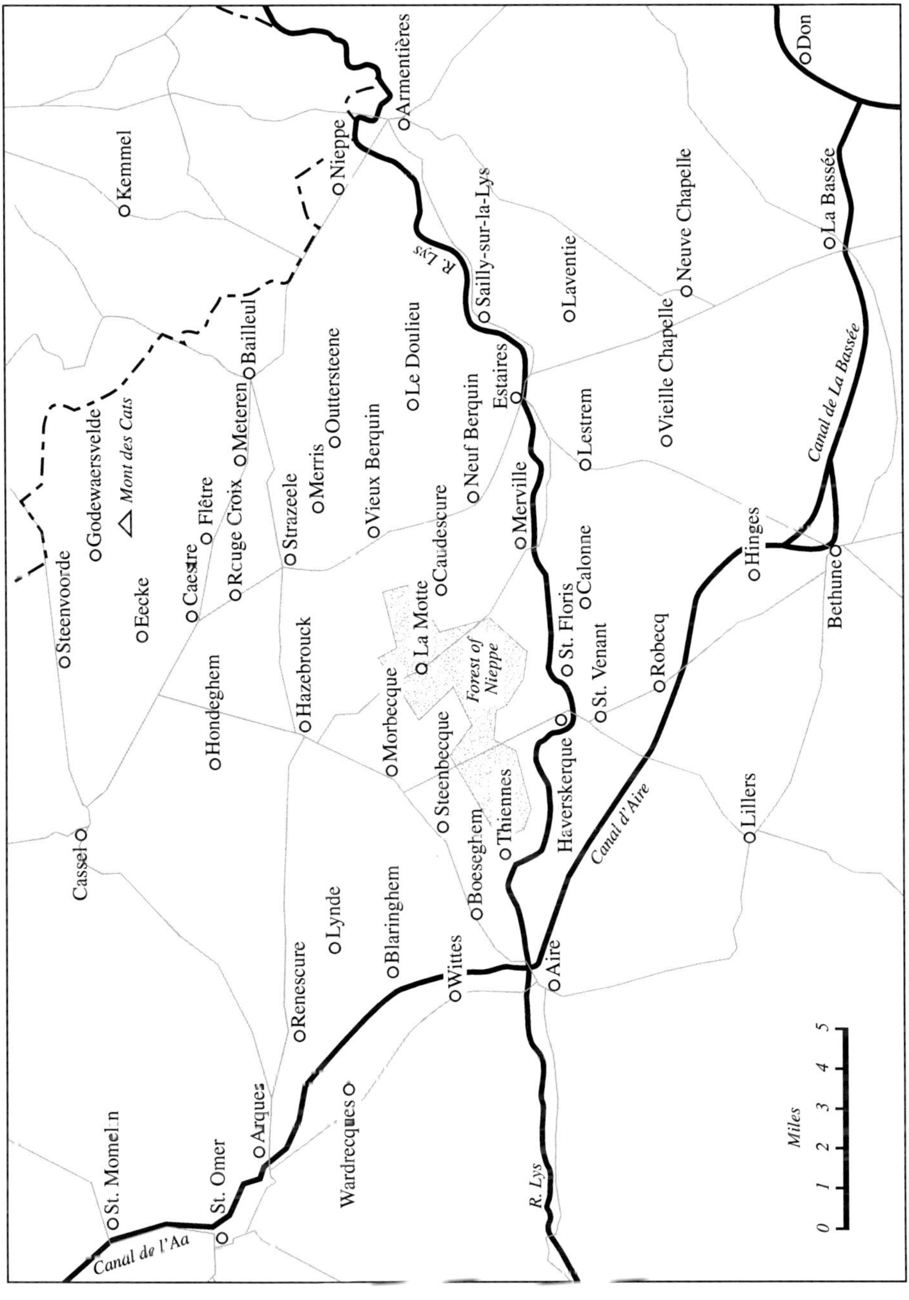

CHAPTER 7

The Canal Line

While the fierce battle for the Escaut had been going on, the situation in the south had become ever more threatening as by midnight on 20 May German armoured spearheads reached the English Channel near Abbeville. This effectively cut the Allied forces in two and laid bare the southern flank of the BEF. Lord Gort organised a counterattack the next day south of Arras using the tanks of 1st Army Tank Brigade and an infantry brigade of 50th Division. Although its success was limited, the action both delayed the enemy's advance and made them more cautious by confirming fears of the vulnerability of their own extended flanks as the armour raced forward leaving the infantry struggling to keep in touch.

The BEF set about establishing a defensive line along the natural barrier of canals stretching from the coast through St Omer, Béthune and La Bassée. A number of improvised forces, sometimes ill-equipped and weak in supporting arms, were hastily organised to occupy it. By the 23rd, as more troops had been progressively made available, the units were disposed with Usherforce on the right along the Aa canal to the sea and Polforce on the left.[(1)] Polforce was spread out over some 48 miles from Raches to Watten, with 25th Infantry Brigade covering the bridges on either side of La Bassée and 137th Infantry Brigade, initially with just one battalion, responsible for all the crossings from Hinges, west of Béthune, to the junction with Usherforce. At the same time, Macforce was moving up towards the Forest of Nieppe and Woodforce was organising a garrison for Hazebrouck, where General Headquarters had taken refuge. With the forces available, all that could be hoped for was that the principal canal crossings could be held until the divisions being freed from the main eastern front arrived to take over the defence of the line.

The first German armour and infantry reached the line opposite St

Omer during the night of 22nd/23rd and the following day secured the main bridge in working order despite attempts by the British engineers to demolish it. At other crossings in the sector, the small detachments defending them were also either overrun or driven back and by the end of the day's fighting the enemy had a fair sized bridgehead in the area St Omer – Renescure – Lynde. The units of Polforce in this sector took up fresh covering positions at Morbecque, Steenbecque and Boeseghem.

For the moment 44th Division was to be held in General Headquarters reserve, but along with the 2nd and 48th Divisions it would be switched to take over the defence of the Canal Line as soon as possible. As some of the consequent reliefs and movements could not be carried out until the night of the 23rd/24th the divisions were each ordered to find a small force of mainly gunners and machine gunners to hurry down in advance to the threatened sectors.

Back at Oudenmolen, the Regiment received verbal orders at 11 a.m. on the 23rd to proceed to Sailly-sur-Lys, north of La Bassée, the War Diary adding perhaps somewhat optimistically: 'presumably for re-fitting'. The Second-in-Command, Major G.P. Chapman, went ahead with a reconnaissance party to get things ready. Everyone was very tired after being in action and the day was spent in catching up on some sleep and getting something to eat, while trying to avoid the attention of low-flying German aircraft. In the afternoon news was received that 50 reinforcements were on the way and transport was sent to meet them.

Then at 8 p.m. an urgent message was received from Major Chapman that the Regiment was to join Polforce immediately as the Germans were pushing towards Hazebrouck from the west in an attempt to widen their salient. Regimental Headquarters was to be established in Sailly sur Lys while the batteries were to be dispersed as follows: 227 and 228 Batteries with a total of 16 guns were to report to 137th Infantry Brigade at Morbecque; 225 Battery with 11 guns was to report to 25th Infantry Brigade situated at Don; and 226 Battery with 7 guns was to go to Sailly-sur-Lys as a mobile reserve. The message added that the batteries were to proceed with the utmost speed and at 9.15 p.m. the Regiment got underway with the newly arrived reinforcements allocated to the batteries as they passed en route.

The long and tiring drive through the night took the Regiment on the same route as that on which it had advanced triumphantly into Belgium less than two weeks before, but now the situation was more serious. The roads were again congested and there were frequent halts, where the drivers struggled to keep awake and inevitably the column got split up. 227 and 228 Batteries had the furthest to go and moved on through Sailly-sur-Lys towards the Forest of Nieppe and Morbecque. A long straight road cut right through this thick forest and as the batteries emerged on its northern edge they were confronted with the evidence of recent shelling. It was about 2.30 a.m. when Captains Abbott and Hampton reported to Brigadier J.B. Gawthorpe, commanding 137th Brigade, at his headquarters at Morbecque Chateau. Captain Hampton recalled: 'Things were in a bit of a state... and the chateau had been bombed and shelled. We were tired out and hungry but we had to attend a conference immediately. Graham and I both fell asleep! However not much affected us and at about 4 a.m. we left. The guns and trucks had all arrived and were hidden.'

It was discovered, however, that three guns from 227 Battery had gone missing at a roadblock in Armentières. One rejoined the Battery at Morbecque and was put straight into action, but the two others from H Troop attached themselves to the 5th Royal Horse Artillery and remained in action with them until the guns were withdrawn to Dunkirk where they were destroyed. The two gun teams were H1 under Sergeant V. Smith and H3 under Bombardier W. Dalton.

Regimental Headquarters reached Sailly-sur-Lys around 4 a.m. and established itself close to Polforce Headquarters amidst the congestion of guns and transport in the village.

In addition to the anti-tank guns of the Regiment, more infantry, machine gunners, field guns and the light armour of two divisional reconnaissance regiments had arrived or were on their way, prompting

Brigadier Gawthorpe to believe that for the first time he had a force sufficient to introduce some vigour into the defence. It was just as well, as the German panzers started early on Friday 24 May to expand their bridgehead.

Captain Hampton provided a vivid description of the morning's events: 'This was to be the finest day of 228 Battery where the men proved themselves. I had something to eat. I did not bother to sleep. Just before 7 a.m., I was sent for by the Brigadier. A German tank attack was coming in from the north and evidently heading for Morbecque. "See what you can do about it, but you will have to be quick," said the Brigadier. There was no time to be lost. Troop Commanders arrived at once - no time for proper orders: J Troop, two guns up this road and two up here; K put a gun up there and take two up through that wood and see what happens; L you go back here and protect the 25 pounders; B.H.Q. will remain here - I will come up with you shortly in front - any questions? O.K. off you go. Those were my orders and I remember them to this day. Away went the guns and after leaving George Golding who was now my No.2 in charge, I went along after the guns to see what was happening. Some guns got a bit mixed but I sorted them out and we then waited. I was up a road on a hill to the north of Morbecque.

'The light tanks came up and stopped some yards behind me, also waiting. Graham Abbott had got his guns up in front too, he was very fine and took his orders from me without question, personally seeing his guns into position.

'Soon I saw a distant farm house go up in flames, then another. Machine gun fire, fairly close now, light shell fire probably from guns in the tanks, then I thought I could hear tank motors. The ridge in front had a wood on top and I could not see much. The noise increased and continued - they were coming, but what was their direction? It was very puzzling. They were advancing very slowly. It certainly seemed as if they were not coming our way after all, and then in a flash I saw our danger. They were going into Hazebrouck on our right and I had not put guns as far over as that. I immediately withdrew two guns from the left and sent them round to the threatened flank, telling the commander exactly where I wanted them. All my dispositions had to be taken from the map. I went back to Morbecque, told the Brigadier what was happening and went off to the right. I met Graham who had bad news. One of his guns and two of mine had run slap into a tank as they came out of a wood in front. Two had been destroyed, with casualties, including an officer of Graham's. I then met my survivors with a gun. Poor fellows, their nerves had gone temporarily. They would not man the gun - it was suicide - the Sergeant was a good fellow so he and I said we would take their places. They immediately manned their gun and I stayed with them for the rest of the morning. From our position we could see what was happening in the open ground down on the right. There were the German tanks, practically stopped, shooting like fury. Our guns had arrived just in time and were taking them on - our tanks were helping them. It was a thrilling sight - we were giving them shot for shot - two German tanks were caught and blew up in a great sheet of flame and clouds of smoke.

'A British tank suffered a similar fate - there were about eight German tanks there. One of them saw us watching this so he started his own strafe - without any result - although his shooting was accurate. When he had finished, we carried on watching and to our intense delight, the Germans were withdrawing - so we had beaten them there. I stayed up a bit longer and then wandered back to my H.Q. I was amazed to see that the time was after midday.'[(2)]

The gun detachment that put the two tanks out of action was Bombardier H. Bosman's of J Troop. After the leading tank was knocked out at a distance of 1,000 yards, the detachment came under heavy shell and small arms fire from the remaining tanks. A second tank was then hit and put out of action, together with a third that was able to manoeuvre in the rear of the gun position. The gun was eventually damaged by fire from the tanks, mortally wounding Bombardier Bosman, seriously injuring another man and also wounding Lance Bombardier E. Stredwick. Captain Hampton initially recommended the whole team for immediate gallantry awards, but finally selected Lance

Bombardier Stredwick to receive the Military Medal. A British tank brought the gun back

Second-Lieutenant R.W. Smith-Stafford, commanding G Troop, was the officer casualty in 227 Battery when some guns ran straight into the German tanks while taking up position. Gunner Ken Johnson, driving the gun tower, recalled: 'Our gun and the troop commander were in the lead. We rounded a corner in the wood and saw tanks ahead of us and neither the officer nor I could identify if they were friend or foe. The officer dismounted, drew his revolver and walked towards the tanks whereupon a machine gun opened up and he fell to the ground. I baled out of the truck into the ditch alongside the road.'

At the same time, the gun was being manhandled into the emergency firing position on its wheels as Joe Courtney described: '… by means of the handspike the gun was turned around. I was in the gun layer's seat and Jock [Gunner T. Tenant] had rammed home a shell, when out in front strode our officer, pistol in hand. He hadn't gone far when a hail of machine gun bullets cut him down. After getting over the surprise all hell was let loose. Guns swung in our direction and a salvo of high explosive shells descended on us. The first to cop it was the 15 cwt with all the ammunition and our equipment. We all dived into the narrow ditch as enemy shells mixed with our own started to explode sending bits of jagged casing screaming overhead. Now their machine guns started chattering away sending bits of dirt onto our helmets. We set off crawling the way we came.'

The Germans also attacked south of the forest swinging eastwards towards Merville and attempted to cross one of the canal bridges, but were halted by an anti-tank rifle of the 6th King's Own covering it. 226 Battery was sent forward from Sailly-sur-Lys to Merville and took up positions on the edge of the deserted aerodrome south of the town. There were several burnt out British and French planes on the aerodrome and immense stores of abandoned ammunition and petrol. A mix-up occurred with tragic consequences when three French tanks approached the Battery with their guns pointing towards them. They failed to give the proper recognition signals and with enemy tanks known to be in the area, they were engaged and knocked out at very short range.[3] During the action the gallant Second-Lieutenant Edwards was mortally wounded and evacuated to a field hospital.

Another determined effort made by the enemy this day was in the Béthune area where they attempted to cross the La Bassée canal in the sector held by the 25th Brigade. The most serious attack was repelled by the 1st Royal Irish Fusiliers and elsewhere the enemy was no more successful, although the area was heavily shelled throughout the day. 225 Battery, was one of a number of additional units that arrived in support of the brigade, but unfortunately it is not possible to establish from the available records if it was in action.

As the day drew to a close the ever present threat posed by the enemy tanks remained. At Morbecque, two 2-pounders from 228 Battery were deployed with some field guns around 137th Brigade Headquarters in response to an expected incursion.[4] Captain Hampton wrote: 'The Germans were shelling the village, and their infantry had got close enough to drop mortar bombs... There was the hell of a noise going on and then someone, one of the retreating infantry, said the tanks, Germans ones, were coming in at the other end of the village. Five 25 pounder field guns were immediately placed in position on the crossroads outside the chateau, and I put in two of my own guns. And there we waited - gun loaders with shells in their hands ready to whip into breaches, layers in their seats with eyes glued through telescopes, gun commanders standing behind their guns with fire orders ready and the few remaining officers standing by the guns. We knew this was a "last round last man" show - and the opening range as the tanks came round the corner would be less than 100 yards.' The attack did not materialise, however, and after what seemed like an eternity, the field guns limbered up to pull out and the 2-pounders were ordered to do likewise.

The decision had been taken to get all the available guns in 227 and 228 Batteries back to Sailly-sur-Lys where Regimental Headquarters was established. On arrival they were ordered back into action at La Motte, a small village in the heart of the Forest of Nieppe, to where Brigadier Gawthorpe had moved his headquarters as Morbecque was no longer tenable as a suitable location. Preceded by 227 Battery, it was quite dark by the time 228 arrived and having disposed the guns as best as they could they settled down to sleep – their first for three nights.

At Merville, 226 Battery, taking advantage of a mobile kitchen left behind by The Royal Air Force on the aerodrome, sent out foraging parties who rounded up enough vegetables and chickens for everyone to have a good meal. This was just as well as the BEF had been put on half rations the previous day and food would be increasingly hard to come by in the days that followed.

It had been a costly day for the Regiment. In addition to the officer casualties mentioned, three men had been killed, 16 wounded, some seriously, and another 27 were missing. On a brighter note Captain Hampton was awarded a Military Cross for his 'exceptional initiative and boldness' in dealing with the tank attack. That it was well deserved is illustrated by the fact that there were three separate recommendations: by Brigadier Gawthorpe of 137th Brigade; by Major-General H.O. Curtis of Polforce; and by Lieutenant-Colonel Travers. Captain Abbott was also recommended for the award, but as the authorities decreed that only one could be given for the action, he had to settle for a Mention in Despatches.

With the arrival of the divisions designated to hold the Canal Line, all the improvised forces were abolished as of 3.a.m. on Saturday 25th and in the afternoon the Regiment returned to the command of 44th Division. Together with the 2nd and 46th Divisions, the 44th was responsible for the southern front along the Canal Line, with a brigade of 48th Division also allocated for the defence of Cassel. I and II Corps continued to hold the British sector of the frontier line facing east, while III Corps concentrated for an Anglo-French counterattack southwards on the 26th. When the orders for this attack were cancelled, the 5th and 50th Divisions moved to the left of the eastern front where a serious German attack had driven back the Belgian Army.

Map 4: The Forest of Nieppe

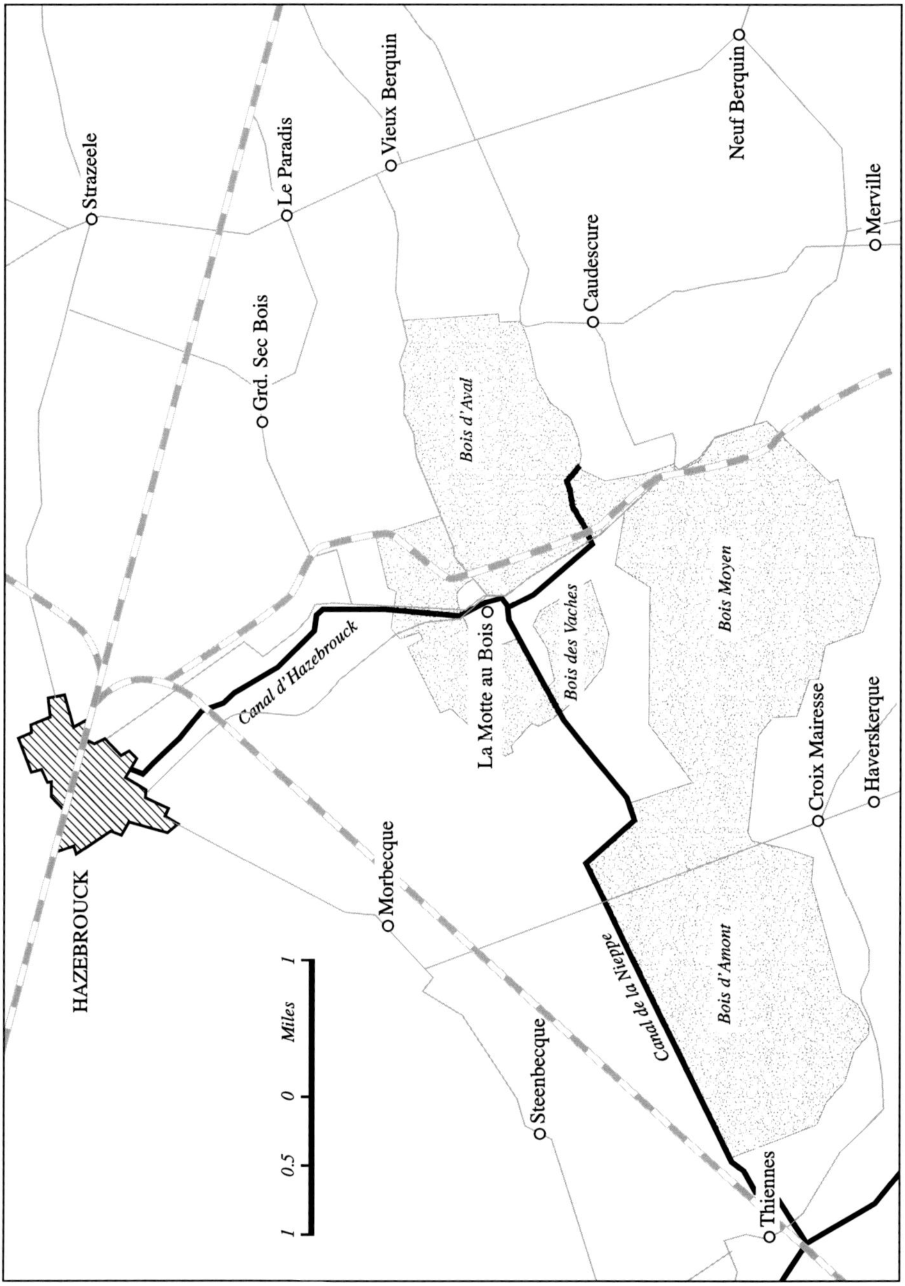

This regrouping of the BEF was in part enabled by a lull in the German advance resulting from an order that its armoured forces should be halted on the Canal Line for maintenance and to conserve them for any future operations. The overall situation of the BEF and its allies in the north continued to deteriorate, however, as they were confined within a shrinking perimeter facing the enemy on three points of the compass and with their backs to the sea. With Boulogne captured and Calais closely invested, Dunkirk remained as the only port through which they could be supplied or evacuated.

On the Canal Line, 44th Division deployed with 132nd Brigade on the left in the Forest of Nieppe, taking over from 137th Brigade, and with 133rd Brigade on the right north-east of Hazebrouck at Caestre. On arrival 131st Brigade was to be in reserve, but was later brought forward to Strazeele.

Regimental Headquarters moved to a new location at Les Trois Fermes close to Divisional Headquarters at Ecole de Steentje, south of Bailleul. 225 and 226 Batteries found themselves back at Outtersteene, although a section of two guns of the latter remained at Merville under Lieutenant R. Wealleans. 227 and 228 now formed a composite battery of 11 guns with its headquarters at La Motte. The depleted number of guns in the composite battery included two damaged guns recovered from the previous day's fighting and one from another regiment found abandoned after its crew had become casualties.

During the day and into the night, 132nd Brigade re-occupied the high ground that had been lost west of Morbecque and Steenbecque without meeting any opposition. In addition to the composite battery, six guns of 225 Battery were placed in support of the brigade and early next morning 226 Battery joined the 4th Royal Sussex of 133rd Brigade to bolster the defence of Caestre.

As a result of the halt order no serious enemy attacks were made over the weekend, but there were many local actions as German units developed their positions. Reports of infiltration by German tanks necessitated the frequent movement of the Regiment's guns, but no tanks were seen and the situation generally remained obscure. As one gunner summed it up, 'If there was someone who knew what was going on, he was not telling us.' Bombed and shelled continuously, the strain on the men's nerves began to tell.

The dark interior of the forest also heightened the feeling of isolation and made it difficult to identify friend from foe. Rumours abounded that the Germans were everywhere. Joe Courtney recalled: 'We now found ourselves digging in the area of a large, foreboding thick forest. We felt dreadfully exposed and alone, the dense forest to our right looked uninviting, and I had a premonition that danger lurked there... In the distance could be heard the clanking of tank tracks.'

The 26th was a Sunday and the BBC news reported that it was a national day of prayer for the safety of the BEF, which as Captain Hampton commented: '...came as a great surprise to us all. We knew things were not going as well as one might wish, but it would surely all work out in the end.'

During a lull, Captain Hampton took an armed party to the dressing station at Morbecque to check on the condition of the wounded and there they found Bombardier Bosman dead on his stretcher. The description of his burial can perhaps stand as a testament to the many like it that went unrecorded. 'We dug his grave in the front garden of the nearby farm and laid him to rest, marking the spot with a wooden cross,' wrote Captain Hampton. 'Of course, the one time I needed it, I had left my booklet which gave instructions back at La Motte, so we just recited the Lords Prayer and went home - very sad and rather tear-jerking.'(5)

Throughout the day the defensive outposts on the western edge of the forest were attacked and the enemy gained a foothold in Morbecque. During a reconnaissance in the Bois de Huit Rues, north-west of Morbecque, it was reported to Second-Lieutenant R.G. Orr of 225 Battery that an enemy tank had been seen in the corner of the wood. Unable to get his 2-pounder gun into action against the tank because of the trees, he armed himself with an anti-tank rifle borrowed from the infantry and went to track it down. The tank was found to be in a hastily constructed 'hide-out' and manoeuvring into a favourable position to engage it, he fired eight rounds. Five of them were direct hits and the tank burst into flames. Second-Lieutenant Orr was awarded the Military Cross.

In the afternoon, Regimental Headquarters was informed that there were some 2-pounder guns without command on the main road north of Caestre towards Eecke. Major Chapman was sent to site these guns which proved to be two in number.

The German efforts died down at dusk, but there was a feeling that they were building up for a strong attack and during the night the panzers could be heard assembling to the south.

South of the Forest of Nieppe, 44th Division had linked up with the 2nd Division whose right-hand brigade, the 6th, took up positions forward of the Lys Canal in the St Venant - Robecq sector. Before dawn on 27 May the centre of the division was subjected to a vicious bombardment and by about 8.00 a.m. the onslaught had spread to the 6th Brigade. Tanks rolled over the forward positions and the few supporting anti-tank guns available did their best, but were knocked out by the weight of fire. The brigade held out until midday when it was ordered to withdraw, but only a remnant managed to escape over the canal bridges and seek refuge in the forest.

East of St Venant the armoured columns advanced on Merville, where the two guns of 226 Battery were swept up in the assault. Driver Sid Harris recalled: 'We could see through the mist and hear the rumbling of German tanks coming down the road. As I was the driver, I helped to load the gun and our team started firing at the tanks. Then an enormous burst of firing, bullets and shells were whistling and landing all around us. We still kept on firing at the tanks and put at least three out of action. Cecil Chandler and myself went to my truck to get some more ammunition and a shell came over and landed near our gun killing three of the crew and the gun was damaged. We were both dazed, but decided to get our rifles and crawl through the ditches and hedges to the next farmhouse.' After joining in a rearguard action the pair were taken prisoner as was the section commander Lieutenant Wealleans. Merville did not fall, however, and the 6th King's Own gallantly held the Germans back all through the day.

In the Forest of Nieppe continuous heavy pressure was brought to bear on 132nd Brigade, now with both 225 Battery and the composite 227/228 under command. Outposts on the south-western edge of the forest, known as the Bois d'Amont, were strongly attacked by infantry of the SS Verfügungs (General Service) Division. They were a formidable enemy comprised of armed units of the Schutzstaffel, better known as the SS, who were originally created as Hitler's personal bodyguard. The men were carefully selected, highly trained, well equipped, ideologically motivated and carried out their tasks in a tough and aggressive manner. After the campaign in France, the SS Verfügungstruppen would be the cornerstone of the future elite Waffen (Armed) SS divisions. The Division deployed with the Regiment 'Der Führer' on the left and the Regiment 'Germania' on the right. With artillery and Stuka dive-bomber support, the attack made rapid progress on the open left flank through Steenbecque and Morbecque, but in the forested area of the Bois d'Amont it met stiff resistance. The positions were held by the 5th Royal West Kent supported by guns of 225 Battery. German battle reports stated that the area was defended vigorously, but the SS pressure was too strong to be held indefinitely. By 10 a.m. they had penetrated the main battalion position along the road running north-west from Haverskerque to Morbecque. A counterattack using carriers checked the Germans for a while, but by the early afternoon it had become evident that the position was untenable and the battalion withdrew to La Motte au Bois.

Under orders to remain in position and left isolated by the sometimes precipitate infantry withdrawals, the gun detachments were again faced with being bombarded and overrun or pulling out in the nick of time. The German Reconnaissance Battalion moving either side of the Canal de Nieppe, on the northern edge of the wood, reported it had captured two anti-tank guns and a number of trucks and men. Driver Jack Boswell of 225 Battery graphically described his detachment's experiences: 'We took up positions on the edge of the forest and were told to expect tanks shortly. That was on 26 May and during the night exhausted troops streamed through our positions. We settled down to wait for the attack that we thought would be at dawn. Daylight came and the expected tanks did not arrive, but shells began to fall about five hundred yards to our right. Our number two gun was somewhere in that area and my pal Tommy Catton was the layer. I wondered if they had been spotted by the Germans. Suddenly we saw a figure staggering towards us. It was the Sergeant off that gun and he had a large wound in his back caused by a shell splinter. While we were trying to make him comfortable several soldiers came out of the trees to see what was going on. Our Number One, very nervous now, shouted to them to get down before we were spotted. The truck from the other gun arrived in a hurry. The driver told us that the gun had been knocked out, the Sergeant had been wounded and two others killed. The wounded Sergeant was lifted onto the truck and our Sergeant was considering whether to pull out or not when suddenly we were saturated with mortar and machine gun fire. We were taken completely by surprise by the suddenness and ferocity of the onslaught. Ginger Collyer and myself being several feet from the gun dropped to the ground instinctively behind the base of a large tree. Meanwhile John Sullivan and Gunner Blackmore were working the two pounder like madmen. Fortunately I had hold of a .303 [Lee-Enfield rifle] when I fell and Collyer could reach the Bren gun and we let Jerry have everything we had. There wasn't a tank in sight, but the concentrated fire kept their heads down and they backed off a little. Then they gave us another mortar stonk and suddenly I felt a great blast in my back and I was thrown bodily against the tree trunk and must have passed out. When I came to I felt something warm trickling down my back and thought that I must have a large wound like the Sergeant, but luckily it turned out to be a flesh wound. I rolled over to try and get my webbing off to see what damage had been done and there was a Jerry standing over me pointing a rifle. I slowly got to my feet expecting to be shot when I saw Collyer was already standing, blood was pouring from his arm as he had received a bullet through his elbow. Gunner Blackmore's face was purple and covered with spots of blood. Apparently the emergency ammunition container in the gun had been hit setting off the shells inside and he had caught some of the blast. The gun layer John Sullivan was lying still on the ground. He had received terrible wounds to both legs and arms. I looked around and saw that nearly all the men who had joined us before the attack were lying dead or wounded. A German medic attended to the walking wounded and the more seriously wounded were made comfortable until transport was available.

'A senior German N.C.O. then came to speak to us in perfect English. He did not ask the questions we expected and seemed to know more about troop movements and positions than we did. He told us to go forward in front of his men towards the British lines. We looked at each other and all had the same thought, as soon as we were spotted we would stand a good chance of being shot by our own side. Somebody suggested that we swop addresses in case anything happened. None of us had any paper so I took the last of my cigarettes out of an 'Army Club' packet and tore it into several pieces. At that moment a Jerry medic came over and asked if he could have us to help carry two of the less badly wounded to the German R.A.P. [Regimental Aid Post]. The senior N.C.O. agreed and we breathed a sigh of relief. I set about making a makeshift stretcher with my greatcoat and a couple of tree branches, then we had a terrible job carrying the wounded down a narrow track through the woods which was ankle deep in mud. Finally we reached the R.A.P. tent where a German M.O. [Medical Officer] was tending to one of their wounded. That was our introduction to a long spell as prisoners of war, but that is another story.'

Gunner Geoffrey Parker was one of the lucky ones who did get away. Having disabled their gun in the face of approaching German infantry, he went on: 'We made our way on foot to Joe Leary's gun less than half a mile down the road. He was in the open on the edge of the woods. I told him that we had been chased out and so they hooked up. Wormald was driving, but all of a sudden Jerry fired through the hedge as they could see the truck canopy. Bullets went into the engine, caught Wormald's legs and Joe in the arm, but missed me. I said to Joe, come on let's get you out, but he said to leave him as we couldn't do anything. We made our way back to troop headquarters on foot and were told to withdraw.'

Another successful withdrawal was made by Gunner Walter Messenger who earned a Military Medal in the process. The citation records: 'On 27 May this man was Number 3 of a gun sited at the south-west corner of the Forest de Nieppe. A large column of enemy infantry were seen advancing towards his gun position, flanked by machine guns. Fire was opened on his gun position from about 200 yards range, and Gunner Messenger was immediately wounded in the hand and leg. In spite of his wounds he remained at his gun, and continued firing at the advancing enemy. This had the effect of temporarily silencing the enemy's machine guns, and held up their advance. When nearly surrounded and forced out of their gun position, Gunner Messenger together with the whole of his gun crew, withdrew to their vehicles and got away safely.'

On the north-western edge of the forest, the assault by tanks and infantry of the 8th Panzer Division and part of the 6th Panzer Division began by wiping out an isolated company of the 2nd Royal Sussex in the Bois de Huit Rues and then concentrated on Morbecque and Hazebrouck. With observation from the church towers the guns of the 58th and 98th Field Regiments were kept firing busily and later engaged tanks over open sights, while the infantry were engaged in fierce street fighting. Working their way round north of Hazebrouck, the tanks also advanced towards the road that ran south-east from Eecke through Caestre and Strazeele.

As the morning wore on there were evident signs of an impending attack at Caestre, where the guns of 226 Battery under Major Christopher were in support of the 4th Royal Sussex. They were subjected to a fairly persistent bombardment and there were reports of an enemy column crossing the road ahead of the level crossing at the north-west end of the village and later tanks approaching from the west. During the afternoon some light tanks were spotted in a nearby copse and flushed by shellfire from the 65th Field Regiment onto the 2-pounders and the 25mm guns of the brigade anti-tank company covering the hedgerows from the outskirts of the village. Six were knocked out and most of their crews taken prisoner.(6)

Bombardier Jack Fuller, commanding a gun team in E Troop, recalled: 'We were in position on a narrow road with a ditch running alongside it and with the gun in a hedge. We also had a Boys anti-tank rifle out on one side. Suddenly we saw these light tanks come out in line abreast across the field on the other side of the road and we opened up on them. We saw the crews scattering and some time later I thought we better go out and see what had happened. The Germans just gave themselves up and came out with their hands up. I gathered some together and they all went into the back of my 15 cwt truck. I took a Luger pistol off one of them and sat on the tailboard pointing it at them while the driver went back to the village.'

South of Caestre, the 5th Royal Sussex barely had time to occupy the neighbouring village of Strazeele before they were engaged in a sharp encounter with tanks that caused considerable casualties before being driven off.(7)

Although the enemy was unsuccessful in these two attacks, by the close of the day's fighting Morbecque had fallen, Hazebrouck was closely invested and the 132nd Brigade only retained the north-east part of the forest around La Motte. To strengthen the line the 131st Brigade had been brought forward in the centre around Strazeele and linked up with the 133rd Brigade on the right between Rouge Croix and Caestre. The dispersal of the batteries remained unchanged with 225 Battery and the composite 227/228 under 132nd Brigade and 226 with the 4th Royal Sussex in 133rd Brigade.

At Les Trois Fermes, Regimental Headquarters had stood to with all available arms in anticipation of an attack, but the main threat came from low-flying air attacks. News of the losses and casualties in all batteries came in throughout the day and there was concern especially for Lieutenant Wealleans section at Merville. In the late afternoon Lieutenant-Colonel Travers was called to a conference at Division and had still not returned by midnight. This fuelled an expectation that the Regiment's departure was imminent and all documents and maps were packed up in preparation. The arrival of a party of Royal Engineers to prepare a small local bridge for demolition added to the expectation and the Regimental transport was moved over the stream to be on the correct side to enable its future withdrawal.

Although the night of the 27th was fairly uneventful, it started to rain hard and continued to do so for some hours doing nothing to help improve the men's weary spirits.

NOTES

(1) The improvised forces mostly bore names derived from their commanders, but Polforce was named after the town of St Pol - the most important locality in the original forward defensive screen 20 miles south of the canal line and intended to be occupied by Polforce.

(2) In a brief history of 137th Brigade, Brigadier Gawthorpe wrote that the German attack 'had been most gallantly checked by a territorial anti-tank battery, formed at Northampton.' The latter is almost certainly a corruption of Captain Hampton's name.

(3) The 137th Brigade history mentions three French tanks that, 'started to shoot up advanced British positions and had to be checked violently'.

(4) The 25-pounders belonged to 392 Battery, 98th Field Regiment (Surrey and Sussex Yeomanry Q.M.R) R.A. (T.A.).

(5) Bombardier Bosman is commemorated on the Dunkirk Memorial as having no known grave. His gun detachment was credited with knocking out the first tank and collected the £5 bounty offered by Lieutenant-Colonel Travers. On returning home Captain Hampton saw to it that this went to his widow.

(6) The 25-pounder guns of 257 Battery, 65th Field Regiment in position at Flêtre claimed to have knocked out two of the tanks.

(7) The history of the 5th Royal Sussex, Cinque Ports Battalion, includes an account of the action stating: 'Two Artillery 2-pounder anti-tank guns, which were in the village, came into action on the road where one was hit.' It is tempting to state that the guns belonged to the Regiment.

Map 5: Retreat to Dunkirk

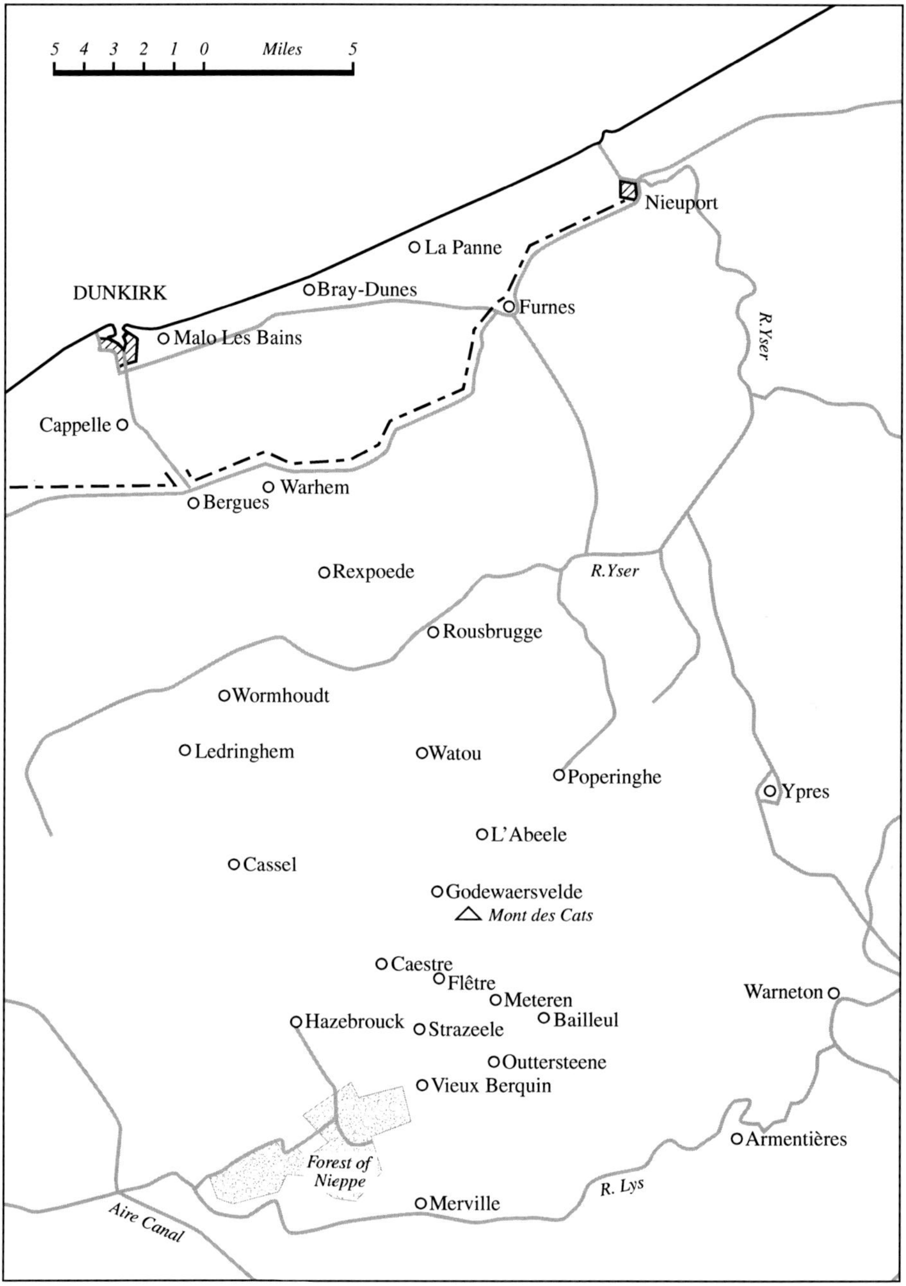

CHAPTER 8

Tumble to the Sea

Operation 'Dynamo' was the code name given to the plan for the evacuation of the BEF from Dunkirk and neighbouring beaches. The planning for such a possible contingency had started a little more than a week after the start of the German attack, initially considering the partial evacuation of non-combatants and some key specialists.(1) As the situation worsened, the reality of a large scale compulsory evacuation was accepted and shortly before 7 p.m. on 26 May the Admiralty sent the signal for it to commence.

This decision had become inevitable as the sustained German attacks pressed the BEF inwards into the pocket within which it was confined. The Belgian front was also crumbling and by midnight on the 27th the King of the Belgians had accepted defeat and ordered a cease fire. This created a twenty-mile open gap on the northern flank of the BEF towards the sea covered only by light mobile forces until the divisions of II Corps could move to fill it.

A defensive perimeter around Dunkirk was established along the canals that ran from Nieuport in the east through Furnes and the fortified town of Bergues to Gravelines in the west. The French were to be responsible for the western half of the perimeter and the British the eastern half, that included the beaches east of Dunkirk and the resorts of Malo les Bains and Bray Dunes in France and La Panne across the border in Belgium. Each of the three corps of the BEF was allotted a sector within the perimeter into which its various divisions would withdraw - with II Corps on the left, I Corps in the centre and III Corps on the right nearest to Dunkirk. To avoid congestion all vehicles were to be disabled and abandoned outside the perimeter, but this order was not always obeyed.

Across the channel an armada of ships was assembled and rushed to the beaches to embark the troops without delay. It was a race against time to save as many men as possible before they were cut-off by the German advance.

In the early hours of the 28th, Lieutenant-Colonel Travers returned from the conference at 44th Division with the following message to send to all batteries: Jettison all equipment and stores - All ranks carry light equipment and all arms and ammunition - Royal Artillery of Division are to cover flank of withdrawal - BEF are withdrawing to the coast.[2] Regimental Headquarters was to move at dawn and establish itself near Divisional Headquarters at Godewaersvelde, north-west of the Mont des Cats. The batteries would move independently under instructions of their respective formations.

Captain Hampton recalled that a dispatch rider arrived at about 4 a.m. with news of the withdrawal and instructions that 225, 227 and 228 Batteries would take part in the rearguard to cover the withdrawal of 132nd Brigade.

The three battery headquarters were moved back to the Vieux Berquin area to be near brigade headquarters, with 228 located at the inappropriately named Le Paradis. Captain Hampton added: 'I sent my B Echelon back to a hide-out near Meteren, behind Bailleul, with orders to wait for me. If they looked like getting captured, they could go back further. George Golding was with them so they were in capable hands.'

The remaining guns of the batteries were in positions in the north-east part of the Forest of Nieppe helping to cover the canal running south-east from Hazebrouck. The Royal West Kent battalions of 132nd Brigade were disposed with the 4th on the right, with its left flank at La Motte au Bois, and the 5th holding the left portion of the canal and its eastern extension the Canal de Pré à Vin. The 1st Battalion was in reserve on the eastern edge of the Bois d'Aval. The gap between the forest and Hazebrouck was covered by the 2nd Royal Sussex who came under command of the brigade.

Tasked with clearing the whole of the forest this day, the Regiments of the SS Verfügungs Division deployed to attack again in the morning. The I Battalion of the Regiment 'Der Führer' reached the Bois des

Vaches before being forced to halt as it came up against the canal defences. The Germans then probed along the whole brigade front and very heavy pressure was brought to bear on the 2nd Royal Sussex from the Hazebrouck direction. A breakthrough was achieved in the afternoon when under the cover of a heavy bombardment the III Battalion of the Regiment 'Der Führer' crossed the canal in rubber boats north of La Motte and then pushed on through the forest and turned to attack the northern edge of the Bois d'Aval. La Motte was entered, lost and then recaptured in a prolonged struggle. Although the attack continued to make steady progress, the Regiment 'Der Führer' reported that the British troops defended very stubbornly and had to be defeated post by post.

On the right, the II and III Battalions of the Regiment 'Germania' pushed slowly through the Bois Moyen hampered by the dense forest and heavy rain that had turned the ground into a quagmire. They reached the eastern edge in the late afternoon and the left (III) battalion thrust north against the British flank. Both the 5th Royal West Kent on the Canal de Pré à Vin and the 1st in its rear reported that they were attacked by infantry and tanks, the latter from the 3rd Panzer Division advancing from the south after Merville had fallen.

The day's events were described by Captain Hampton: 'We were shelled on and off all day and bombed now and again. The Germans were gradually closing in and their tanks were trying to get through. Leslie Goodman killed two of them which was good work. The visibility was poor - foggy. The General visited us in the evening which was very heartening. As time went on, the noise of machine gun and rifle fire increased. The infantry were retreating and our guns had come back to the main roads, and unless something was done pretty soon, it rather looked as if we would be in danger of being cut off. I saw the Brigadier late in the evening and he said he proposed to go back to Flêtre, about five miles back on the road to Dunkirk. He would let me know when. I went back to the men and had a sleep in a barn. The noise was pretty loud now. Some French detachments were making half-hearted attempts to dig themselves in nearby. An hour later when it was getting dark, I was woken up and told the Germans were very close. I went along to see the Brigadier and found that he and his staff had gone. I was in a bit of a quandary - the Germans were on top of us - I had 17 guns - I had no orders - and we were, once more, high and dry. The other two Battery Commanders placed themselves under my orders and wanted to know what to do. Just then Leslie Goodman came up and said that a Colonel of the West Kents ordered us to get out at once.'

As darkness fell the situation of the brigade was precarious and when the orders came through for it to withdraw it was only with some difficulty that the troops were able to break contact with the enemy. They were to make for Flêtre and then join the stream of traffic making its way to Dunkirk. Not all were lucky though and some had their escape routes barred or were forgotten in the confusion. The night was cool and stormy.

The batteries withdrew at about 10.30 p.m., but as Captain Hampton wrote: 'That was easier said than done. We could not go back towards Flêtre, as the Germans were across the road and had cut us off. I decided to go forwards to Vieux Berquin, turn left and go through Outtersteene towards Bailleul, then turn left to Meteren, find our B Echelon and try to contact the Brigadier at Flêtre. We got the guns out, lined up in the road and when everyone was ready, we pushed off. There was no panic or fuss: we all knew we were in a ticklish position and we would have to be very lucky to get out. It was somewhat nerve-wracking, particularly when we were going towards Bailleul. Not far to the south were burning villages, the flashes of guns and shells and all the attendant noise. We did not know if the Germans were across the road in front. I prayed they were not. I sat in my truck with my revolver ready.'

While 132nd Brigade had been fighting in the Forest of Nieppe, 131st and 133rd Brigades struggled to deny the Caestre-Strazeele road to the enemy. The bombardment of Caestre, where 226 Battery remained in support of the 4th Royal Sussex, resumed in the morning and continued fiercely all day with only occasional lulls. Tanks again showed themselves at intervals north-west of the village, but the heaviest attacks were made to the south. During the afternoon the line was broken around Rouge Croix and the situation only restored by a counterattack. Strazeele was also assaulted, but the position was held with the aid of some French tanks.

To the defenders of Caestre, the situation on the flanks remained obscure throughout the day and there was an uneasy concern that they were being encircled. By nightfall it was clear that the road to the south had been cut and Lieutenant-Colonel L.G. Whistler, commanding the 4th Royal Sussex, asked 133rd Brigade with some urgency if the battalion was to remain in position for the night. At the same time he urged Major Christopher to hold tight with the battery's three remaining guns.(3)

At 10.00 p.m. orders came to withdraw through Flêtre to the Mont des Cats, a naturally strong position six miles in the rear. General Osborne had decided that instead of trying to make a long march immediately following such a hard day's fighting, he would move the Division there (less 132nd Brigade already gone) and continue the withdrawal on the following night. As silently as possible, the 4th Royal Sussex slipped away from Caestre taking with it only the essential transport required. The guns of 226 Battery and the 133rd Brigade anti-tank company were to march in the rear, all under command of Major Christopher, leaving at 1.30 a.m.

Moving across country in the darkness units lost touch and by dawn only some elements of the Division had reached the Mont des Cats including two guns of the Regiment.(4) As soon as it became daylight the position revealed itself as a high isolated hill visible for miles and thick with troops. The Germans started at once to attack with artillery and mortars, followed later by intensive dive bombing, which clearly heralded a ground attack. Although there had been an intention to stand and fight, this early and intensive enemy activity persuaded General Osborne to abandon the hill. Shortly before 10 a.m., the troops started to move out in two columns, shelled but not molested by the enemy, and with orders to make their way via Poperinghe to the beaches.

The Regiment started the withdrawal essentially in three organised groups: Regimental Headquarters from Outtersteene; the main gun group comprising 225, 227 and 228 Batteries from Vieux Berquin; and 226 Battery from Caestre. To begin with the groups were able to remain more or less intact, but as soon as they became entangled in the congestion on the roads the transport had to be abandoned and they inevitably got split up into smaller parties. Making their way on foot some of the parties then became separated or lost in the crowds of refugees and many men ended up walking alone or in the company of a few friends.

When forced to abandon the transport the melancholy task of rendering it unserviceable to the enemy had to be undertaken. The trucks were variously set alight or unceremoniously pushed into the ditches and canals, engines were smashed by hammers or left running to eventually seize up and tyres were punctured. The surviving guns were similarly dealt with, breach blocks and firing pins were removed and buried or tossed in the canal, as was the ammunition. A number of firing pins and the valuable optical sights were however brought home. The men made the final march to the beaches taking only their personal weapons, Bren guns and any kit they could carry.

Regimental Headquarters

The first party to go was Regimental Headquarters which had left Outtersteene in the early hours of the previous day. Its movements are recorded in the War Diary which with its brief narrative style helps to capture the tension of the day's events:

0500 - Withdrawal in good order.

0640 - Established adjacent to Godewaersvelde in field under cover of hedges and trees. Maps and documents destroyed.

0905 - Terrific air bombing and machine gunning by German planes. 70 counted in the air at one time. Roads severely damaged. Many whistling bombs by dive bombers.

1130 - Infantry report attack by tanks approaching Godewaersvelde from north-west. Small-arms fire and machine gun fire now very close. We have inadequate defence so the Commanding Officer orders further withdrawal to avoid being cut off. All roads north-west are blocked. We pick up several casualties - wounded.

Eventually arrive at Watou via L'Abeele which received artillery and air attack just after. Main stream of withdrawal is heading for Poperinghe - French and British.

About 1600 - We continued via Rousbrugge and Rexpoede - all towns and villages in flames from bombing.

1730 - Roads hopelessly blocked. We turned north to Warhem then west towards Bergues. Crossed the Canal de la Colme and marched towards the coast. We halted at about Cappelle while Lieutenant-Colonel Travers went to Corps Headquarters for instructions. Plenty of air activity and French anti-aircraft guns retaliated.

2230 - We moved towards the coast again led by the Commanding Officer and eventually crossed another canal. The Medical Officer and his staff and truck remained with Corps.

2350 - We were still marching. Heavy gunfire. Dunkirk in flames and heavy pall of smoke from burning oil lay over in that direction.

The party, which had managed more or less to keep together, reached the dunes shortly before 1 a.m. on the 29th and exhausted, the men fell asleep on the sand. Major Chapman, Captain Robinson and Lieutenant J.C. Elwes set out to establish the possible existence of any boats or rafts.

225, 227 and 228 Batteries

After leaving Vieux Berquin and having become separated in Outtersteene due to the congestion, the main gun group eventually reached Meteren and then halted to get some rest. One gun was involved in an accident en route and so badly damaged that it had to be destroyed. The column got underway again about 4 a.m. choosing to go north to Poperinghe, as it was felt that the situation on its left seemed more dangerous. The group included Captain Hampton's 228 Battery, Captain Abbott with the three remaining guns of 227 Battery, and Captain Foulger's 225 Battery bringing up the rear.

Captain Hampton continued: 'The retreat to Dunkirk had begun and I personally did not think we should get through the ever-tightening German net. Every man had orders to make for Dunkirk, each man for himself with the guns.

'The fun started at once. Within a few minutes, we were with the French Army who were also withdrawing. The roads were a solid mass of vehicles, guns, tanks, horses and men. I expected the German air force to find us at any moment. Progress was about a mile per hour to begin with and we had over 30 miles to go. I have often read of armies in retreat and had already retreated myself from Belgium, but that was conducted in an orderly way. This was a headlong retreat of the worst kind imaginable…

'Just before Poperinghe, at about 11 a.m., we had done 12 miles, the aeroplanes came over but attacked a French column on our left. Our progress was still bad, although in Belgium it had become a little easier. War material had already started to be abandoned and we were 20 miles from Dunkirk. On the outskirts of Poperinghe, we were shelled very accurately from the Belgian side, i.e. from our right. After waiting for this to die down, we moved on into the centre of the town, already badly damaged by shells and bombs. Again, the German aeroplanes came over, and gave us hell… I took shelter in a shop - it had no roof, having been hit already. When the aeroplanes had exhausted their efforts, we got going again, by leaps and starts. It took us two hours to get through Poperinghe. On the northern outskirts, we were shelled again, this time from the French side. It was now that I practically abandoned all hope of getting through. The Germans must be all round - were they in front? I was very tired, very dirty, and very shaken, but keep on we must. I had to get the guns back to Dunkirk and get some orders. The scene of carnage was terrible, death was everywhere. We took an alternative route, and managed to get along a bit better, through Watou which had been badly bombed shortly before. Away in the distance we could see a tremendous black cloud in the direction of Dunkirk. "Looks as if it's going to rain", someone remarked. As we got closer, we saw it to be an enormous cloud of smoke. It was simply terrific - Dunkirk was burning - all the oil and petrol was on fire, making it like night.

'We plugged steadily on - every mile further meant less to walk. Approaching Rexpoede, we came across abandoned equipment, guns of every size from 60-pounders to Brens, lorries from 8-ton tractors to small Austin cars, ambulances and store trucks - millions of pounds of it - dead horses and animals.

'Rexpoede had been bombed and mined with horses dead in the streets - a very unpleasant sight. Progress was becoming very difficult now - the roads being littered with abandoned vehicles, men marching, men riding horses - everyone making for Dunkirk. I began to wonder whether I would find the Colonel or Brigadier at Dunkirk as there was no organisation here, and we had only a dozen miles or so to go. We had seen defensive positions in the course of construction a mile back, but nothing formidable and only a few troops. German aeroplanes were circling overhead, but for some reason they never tried to bomb us, and we were an admirable target. We could see Dunkirk now over the Bergues Canal as the land is very flat. Finally, in taking a short cut we drove into a cul-de-sac and could not get out so, 10-11 miles from Dunkirk, I abandoned my vehicle, snatched up my soft hat and with Graham Abbott, George Golding, my B.S.M. and batman, we set off on foot. It was now about 6 p.m. on 29th May. Gunfire was to be heard in the west towards Calais. We struck off across some fields and came to Warhem. The inhabitants were there and seemed quite unconcerned. We were very tired, hungry and thirsty, having had only some dry biscuits and water all day. By the canal at Bergues, I was surprised to see one of my own battery trucks being driven by a total stranger, and full of men. I stopped them and joined them for a lift, and off we went clinging to the sides like a lot of monkeys. There was a fearful jam on the bridge over the canal at Bergues, burning vehicles were off the side of the road. It was now getting dark, chiefly owing to the smoke pall. Within a few minutes of going over, four Heinkels attempted to blow the bridge up. They persevered for some time with no result so far as could be seen. Just short of Dunkirk, a British soldier was shouting out, "British Army to the beaches, French Army to the port." So that was that - no possibility now of finding anyone in authority to get orders.'

The 227 War Diary recorded that Dunkirk was reached at 8 p.m. and that the Battery had been completely dispersed en route and all vehicles and guns were destroyed as the roads became impassable. The good news was though that the majority of the B Echelon and gun group personnel had arrived earlier and more were with Captain Foulger's rear party. Some of their individual stories, which must stand for the many others that went untold, follow:

'On the retreat we had to destroy what guns we had left. We removed all the firing mechanisms, punctured the wheels... The transport, everything was destroyed and from then on you were on your feet. I don't know how many miles we walked, but the roads were clogged with refugees... You couldn't organise marching or keep your troop together, it was just an impossibility and it was more or less on his own that every man made his way to Dunkirk.'

Troop Sergeant Major Aubrey 'Nobby' Ross, H Troop

'The remaining two guns and all the vehicles were destroyed in a field, it was pitiful to see. We punctured the tanks and set light to the whole lot. The wirelesses we dropped down a well. All much to the disgust of the locals. What remained of my troop and some of the headquarters troop walked to Bray Dunes...'

Troop Sergeant Major George Coldman, I Troop

'Not long after we were told every man for himself and to get rid of all our equipment and throw away the firing mechanisms of the guns. We smashed the truck engines up with a hammer... We were told to get to

Burnt-out and disabled 2-pounders on the retreat to Dunkirk

Dunkirk and I walked with bleeding feet and lousy with fleas. You couldn't move on the roads for refugees. The roads were all open with no cover and when we were strafed we had to dive in the ditches. You took short cuts. We never stayed on the roads if we could help it, because of the Stukas. There were no civilians about, especially if the houses had been bombed. We cut through their gardens and houses, only stopping to look to see if there was anything to eat.'

Gunner Leslie Duke, G Troop

'Approaching the crossroads leading out of Poperinghe it seemed as though the whole population of Belgium was on the move. A French artillery battery of horse-drawn 75mm guns were forcing their way through to go into action in a field. We could only watch in horror as the Stukas, sirens screaming, began bombing the roadway. The refugees panicked and sought cover in the field. The French artillery couldn't move and were caught on the road when the bombs fell amongst them. Horses and men were all mixed up and mutilated, with civilian dead and injured scattered about. We were unable to help the injured, but being gunners we helped the French man-handle their guns in position, staying with them most of the afternoon. Before we left, we shook hands with the French Officer. I had the feeling that his battery of guns were making their last stand. Still keeping to the road and scanning the sky for enemy aircraft, the black smoke was getting nearer and nearer. We approached the canal and the bridge that led into Dunkirk. We were dumbfounded at the sight before us. On either side of the road piled high were thousands of vehicles, trucks, spiked guns of all sizes, in fact most of the BEF's equipment.'

Gunner Joe Courtney, G Troop

The story of the 225 Battery B Echelon is told by Captain Gerry Mayberry: 'We were being channeled, voluntarily or not, up towards what turned out to be the road back to Dunkirk. That was the general movement of the traffic. We didn't stop at any particular place that I can remember, although I do recall driving through Poperinghe. Mind you, when I say driving through, it was like Wembley cup final day, the roads were absolutely jam-packed solid with traffic all pointing towards the coast. We got as far as the outskirts of Bergues and then immobilised the vehicles by leaving the engines running until they ran out of petrol and seized up, because you couldn't go any further. We set off on foot for Dunkirk and as there was a lot of enemy dive bombing going on I thought it was stupid that we should be marching in a body of about 50 and making an easy target, so I separated them up into four groups... I had the BQMS of 225 with me, by the name of Blenkinsop and I think when we got to Dunkirk he produced a couple of dozen tins of bully beef from nowhere.'

Driver Stanley Banister of 225 Battery was with a party that went to the Mont des Cats: 'I remember we were on top of the hill... there were lots of troops up there and we were being shelled. Second-Lieutenant Gavin Orr was insistent that we all got in slit trenches and he was marching around when a shell came over and he was wounded in the leg. We got the orders to move... and put him on a 15cwt truck which I drove. We got down [off the hill] and were going along one of the roads, with ditches each side, and these Stukas came and bombed and strafed us. We all got in the ditch and had to get Second-Lieutenant Orr out, because he couldn't walk. Our truck was hit and went up in flames and we lost all our gear.' After finding another vehicle, 'We got almost to the coast until we came to a road which was massed with vehicles - side by side, nose to tail - you couldn't walk through it. I have never seen anything like it. We found a stretcher in one of the vehicles and got Second-Lieutenant Orr on it and walked across the tops of the vehicles!'

226 Battery

While the plan had been for 226 Battery to leave Caestre during the night in the rear of the 4th Royal Sussex, it did not in fact get underway until the following morning. The fate of the B Echelon is told by Battery Quartermaster Sergeant John 'Buster' Brown in his book *In Durance*

Vile: 'On 29th May I was called by the Major at dawn and told to take my men to the coast. News was uncertain: they doubted if Dunkirk or Calais were still clear; if we asked as we went we could not go wrong; Regimental Headquarters had already packed bags and gone home; but the Major would stay until the bitter end.

'We left before 6 a.m. with goodbyes to the gunners, the Sergeant-Major and two officers - all that we now had left. Because no officer could be spared, I would take charge of the convoy. We drove through the village of Caestre, and even at this early hour one of the locals gave us a few parting shots. The village looked eerie in the half light, several buildings bombed out and wallpaper fluttering on gaunt walls. About a mile further on we found a crossroads, where our instructions were to turn right. As a precaution I sent a dispatch rider (D.R.) ahead, telling him to go at least two miles. When he reported back that the road was clear we started once more. Within 300 yards all hell was let loose. The D.R. had been allowed through; we were a much tastier target.

'The windscreen shattered over my head. Behind me our own Bren guns and rifles opened up: our only hope was to drive on. But a lorry headed straight for us. With a crash the two vehicles locked fast. Figures in blue-grey ran around us. Outside the cab door a nasty German pointed a nastier automatic at my head. I reached for my revolver determined to have at least one shot before he killed me. But my driver grabbed my arm. "Don't do that, Quarter. For the sake of us all put your ruddy hands up and surrender! We're hopelessly outnumbered."

'We got out of the truck and had the satisfaction of seeing some German dead. Our Bren guns still spluttered fitfully, but tanks by now appeared; my fighting days were over.

'I looked down the road to see our back lorry reversing and men from the truck in front running to board it. The Germans fired as one man jumped on... The lorry dashed on down the road and round the corner to warn the gun crew of their danger. I later learnt that half of those in that truck were dead when they reached the Major.

'In our party those still alive were lined up against the wall. Six

Germans pointed their Schmeisser guns menacingly at us, while others counted their dead and injured. Quickly I worked out that... thirteen of us were prisoners, and six perhaps escaped by truck... I glanced at our trucks, wrecked and burning at the roadside and remembered all my good friends I'd never see again. The Germans shouted and bawled; for a few minutes it looked as though we would be summarily dealt with.' Later a German officer came over and explained that they would be going on a very long walk - all the way to Germany - and would be held as prisoners of war.

Gunner William 'Jock' Giles jumped onboard the truck that managed to get away. He recalled: 'All hell broke loose... When they opened up on us, everybody baled out... Men were being killed and badly wounded. I saw Bob [Harper] and he was trying to fire with his one arm.(5) Jock Falconer jumped in one of the trucks and turned it round and started to come back. Some men jumped in the back. Bertie Ware was hanging on the side and I was lying on the bonnet with my hand between the two little front windows. This chap came running up along side of me and as he ran the machine gun bullets were coming through the canvas and killed or wounded the men in the back, including one chap holding on to the back who fell off. As we were moving further away the bullets were hitting the ground and ricocheting up and as this lad jumped on next to me he screamed and started slipping. I don't know where you get the strength from but I got hold of his belt and humped him up and we held him there until we finally got away.'(6)

Bombardier Bill Pryse witnessed both the departure and return of the convoy: 'I saw B Echelon driving up the road from the northern end of the village quite early in the morning and they were soon ambushed. Only the last truck, driven by a chap called Falconer, was able to turn and come back and warn us. The remainder of the Battery then grouped in the village square and drove off in the opposite direction. Before long we found the road completely blocked... We were told to split into small groups... The Battery Commander [Major Christopher] and Battery Captain [Captain Sears] led the first group leaving the

Battery Sergeant Major [G. Thomas] to lead the last. My little group went on alone, managed to get a lift part of the way and arrived at Dunkirk as night was falling.'

The missing guns

North-west of Caestre, the road on which the 226 B Echelon had set out ran past the hill on which the fortress town of Cassel stands. Dominating the surrounding countryside it was of vital importance in denying the approaches to Dunkirk. Its defence was in the hands of 145th Brigade, from 48th Division, with light tanks and gunners in support. Among the latter were the two guns of 227 Battery separated from the Regiment on the drive from the River Lys and who had been commandeered by the 5th Royal Horse Artillery (RHA). They had moved to Cassel on 24 May, where three days later the enemy attack got underway.

Gunner Dennis Spink described the team's experiences: 'Cassel was a perfect position as far as we were concerned being on top of a hill and with the RHA dug in behind us. We had very good observation, First World War type trenches and dug-outs and we were quite happy to stay there. There was a long straight road with poplars either side and the main columns of refugees and some troops could be seen quite clearly below us and they were under fairly constant bombing attacks. When an enemy observation plane started circling us, about a dozen Bren guns opened up and shot off his tail, so obviously we weren't alone. However he must have contacted his base before he was shot down, because a few minutes later we received quite a few salvoes of light shells, but we were quite safe in the dug-outs.

'We could hear some tanks moving about down the bottom of the hill, but we didn't see them. After a couple of days of quiet, with only some shelling and machine gunning to the east of us, it came as quite a surprise when we were awakened during the night by engines revving up and lots of noise from the 25-pounder positions. It poured with rain that particular night and Bombardier Dalton went back to find out what was happening, but by the time he returned and we were ready to move the

RHA had gone.[7] Without maps and in the dark it was impossible to follow them. After trying a few blocked roads we eventually came across a column of 25-pounders which had obviously run into an ambush. They had had quite a pounding and if it was the RHA I suppose we were lucky.

'We were now completely lost and slept in a barn overnight, then gradually made our way along whichever road was open, until we suddenly came to the rear of a large column of refugees, troops and ambulances. An officer told us to destroy everything and help stretcher the wounded to Dunkirk about 12 miles away. This was the first we had heard of any evacuation... However, we prepared to carry out orders and I took the firing mechanism from the gun, but then the ambulances started crawling forward. I put the firing mechanism back and we followed the ambulances who obviously had someone in authority clearing their way. We carried on like this for about a day or so making for the pall of smoke which we were told was Dunkirk.

'A couple of miles from Dunkirk the ambulances pulled off the road and we carried on to the outskirts at the western end of the town. At this point there were many troops about and the road in front was completely blocked, so Bombardier Dalton decided to carry on on foot. I again took out the firing mechanism, smashed the sight mounting and then made my way with Gunner Tommy Hyland and Gunner Boxall.'

The team had been lucky to escape from Cassel, as the general orders to retire on the night of the 28th did not reach the garrison until the following morning. When it did start to move at night, the town was surrounded and only a few troops broke through to reach Dunkirk.

NOTES

(1) The Regiment received instructions on 26 May to send four Warrant Officers or Sergeants with qualifications for training to England.

(2) The War Diary mentions that the original was destroyed and that this is the text of the message.

(3) Lieutenant-Colonel L.G. Whistler's Message Book: 28 May, 2025 hrs - Dear Christopher - 5th have left us on our left. I do not know what the answer is yet! Hold

tight.

(4) The two guns were probably from 225 Battery.

(5) Despite being badly wounded Gunner Bob Harper continued firing a rifle with one hand, helping to allow his comrades to escape. His bravery was reported by the survivors in the truck, but nothing more was ever heard of the episode. Luckily he was picked up by a German unit, whose Medical Officer patched up his wounds saving his life. When he reached a rear hospital, the surgeon successfully operated, amputating one leg. He survived to be later repatriated as a prisoner of war.

(6) Among those from 226 Battery who were captured in addition to BQMS Brown were Gunner E. Adney, Gunner R. Harper, Driver J. Henson, Trumpeter D. Hill, Gunner N. Jay and Driver S. Leary. Jack Hill recalled: 'The 13 of us who were captured managed to stick together until we reached the main Stalag No 8B at Lamsdorf. Although we got split up and sent to different working parties, I did come across them at different times.'

Among those known to have been killed in the ambush were Gunner F. Gainey (driving the leading truck), Gunner J. Atkinson, Gunner A. Huxley and Gunner J. Watson. Other members of the battery killed on or around this day were Gunner R. Dixon, Lance-Bombardier H. Evans, Gunner J. Featherstone, Gunner J. Gardner, Gunner R. Grandfield, Lance-Bombardier T. Hanley, Gunner D. Kirlew, Gunner J. Poplett, Gunner J. Ratledge, Lance-Bombardier N. Walters and Gunner A. Yorke.

(7) The 5th Royal Horse Artillery was ordered to move on the night of the 28th to Rexpoede as part of the force to clear up the situation south of Bergues, but got caught up in the congestion on the roads.

CHAPTER 9

Evacuation from Dunkirk

The *Official History* records that by midday on 30 May practically all our retiring forces were within the Dunkirk perimeter. As the last of the divisions entered the bridgehead the enemy followed up quickly and before the day was over they were in close contact with our defences. While this fight to hold back the enemy took place the evacuation of the BEF was now in full swing.

In the order of evacuation, III Corps were to go first and the tired and depleted units of its three divisions, including the 44th, were directed straight to the beaches of Malo-les-Bains on the outskirts of Dunkirk. On arrival they were confronted with an awe-inspiring spectacle. Against a backdrop of drifting black smoke from the burning oil storage tanks west of the port, men stood in long queues on the beaches or on improvised jetties waiting to be ferried by small boats to the larger ships lying off the shore. With the main harbour out of action due to heavy air attacks, other parties of men waited to be lifted from the harbour's long eastern mole (breakwater). This involved a dash along its narrow wooden walkway and then precarious transfer to the ships which braved the wreckage and attentions of the Luftwaffe to come alongside.

As mentioned earlier, Regimental Headquarters had reached the beaches in the early hours of the 29th. After grabbing a couple of hours rest, the party marched along the beach to take its place in a long column of troops waiting to get on the mole. At 5.30 a.m. they boarded the SS Horst, a Dutch schuit taken over a few days previously by a Royal Navy crew.(1)

About one hour later the engines failed as the Adjutant, Captain Tom Robinson, remembered: 'We managed to board a little vessel called the Horst. It was a Dutch boat manned by volunteers from the UK, and we had only just about got off with it very crowded on board, when the engines packed up. The volunteers didn't know about diesel engines, but I had with us our Ordnance Mechanical Officer, Jimmy Elwes. He was completely exhausted and I chucked a bucket of sea water over him and woke him up. I said Jimmy, get down that engine room and see what you can do and he did, he got it going. This was after we had been towed for about an hour by a British trawler.' The Horst eventually reached Margate at about 3 in the afternoon.'

That the boat had broken down and been patched up by Lieutenant Elwes went unnoticed by the weary sleeping men on board as Trumpeter Stan Paul recounted: 'We arrived down at the beach and were told not to stray and to keep together. Eventually we reached the long mole and on the other side of it was a small coal coaster. We eventually got on board and there was a ladder in each corner going down into the hold. We got down into it and looked around and decided we were not stopping there. We made our way back up to the top again and put the Bren gun in a position where we thought we may be able to use it. Unbeknown to us the boat did break down, but we were so tired we couldn't do much about anything. It eventually got started and we made our way to Margate.'

The departure of Regimental Headquarters was relatively swift, but the batteries arriving on the evening of the 29th would have to spend the night or following nights on the beaches and in the dunes behind them. After a slow start, the rate of evacuation was increasing and III Corps had started a system of organising the men into parties of 50 under an officer and allotting serial numbers to denote their turn to embark.

Captain Hampton reached Dunkirk just as an air raid was starting and made his way through smashed and blazing houses to the port and then Malo-les -Bains and the beaches. He wrote: 'An amazing sight met our eyes - down south to the left and beyond Dunkirk, we could see the enormous fires - flames leaping hundreds of feet into the air, with thick black oily smoke. Out to sea were bombed and wrecked ships, including a French destroyer which had received direct hits. Further out was a merchant ship blazing astern. And on the beach itself, thousands of

NYP 68075

Long queues on the Dunkirk beaches

HU1153

Boarding the destroyer HMS Vanquisher from the mole

men. I was immediately put in command of 50 men by an Ordnance Colonel sitting on a shooting stick and told to keep them in the queue. Having sorted them out, I wandered off to see if any of the other men had arrived. It was well after 9 p.m. now. I was glad to find quite a lot of them and they all seemed remarkably cheerful. Ships were expected to take us off that night which cheered me up a lot. I had never seen such a depressing sight as the Allied Armies retreating, and I had had quite enough to last me for some time, and only wanted to get out of all this. Shells were whistling over spasmodically but not landing near us. I went up to the foot of the mole, and found a Naval Officer who said that something had gone wrong with the works and no ships were expected that night.[(2)]

'Resuming my walk back to my 50 men, I passed the wounded, lying on rows of stretchers - some were in a pretty bad way, but I did my best to cheer them up and told them they hadn't long to wait and would be the first to go. I adjusted the bandages of one or two who had head wounds and then went back to find my men. They were all lying in the sand trying to get some sleep - so I followed suit. I spent the rest of the night alternatively trying to sleep, without success, and walking about to keep warm. It was bitterly cold, and my greatcoat was not much protection. About 4 a.m. on 30 May, there were signs of life, so we shook ourselves and formed up in the queue again. The Germans paid us one more visit and bombed Malo-les-Bains, causing further damage to already ruined houses. They then tried to bomb our destroyers which had now arrived, but got driven off by gun fire.

'At 8 a.m. we boarded [the destroyer] H.M.S. Vimy at the mole and immediately cast off. We thanked heaven that there was a sea mist which prevented any unpleasant attentions. How thankful we were to leave that hellish inferno. The Navy looked after us splendidly and gave us hot tea and coffee - the first for days. The decks were crowded with exhausted officers and men. I went down to the boiler room and got warm… At 11 a.m. we reached Dover after an uneventful voyage.'

Captain Mayberry with the 225 Battery B Echelon also departed from the mole: 'We got to Dunkirk and went down to the beach to see what was happening and there was some beach master who said he was doing his best to form people into groups of 50 and would I take my fellows and join that group over there, which I did. We spent the whole of that night there. The group moved forward very slowly until eventually (about 24 hours later) we came up to the mole and there was a destroyer there and we started marching up the jetty, when some Petty Officer yelled at the top of his voice, "what are you bloody well walking for, come on, step on it," because they were under fire. We broke into a run and climbed aboard this destroyer and we came back to Dover.'

On the beaches east of the mole, the men joined the long lines stretching out into the water waiting anxiously for the boats to come. Many found themselves going from one queue to another, while others set out to look for different means of escaping the beaches. All had to endure the constant threat of the Luftwaffe and the shortage of food and water. The following accounts record just some of the many personal stories:

'Eventually we made our way to the beach, and the sight was indescribable. As far as the eye could see, thousands of troops in long lines were disappearing into the sea. The ones in front were standing in water shoulder high, waiting for little boats to take them off the beach. We joined the smallest line, with others forming behind. The weight gradually pushed us deeper into the sea, but as I couldn't swim I thought that I'd rather be shot than drown and so I moved further down the beach.'

Gunner Joe Courtney, 227 Battery

'We got to Dunkirk and tried to get into a queue about a mile long and waited patiently. I felt so damned tired, so I told the blokes around me that I was going to lay down for a while and to give me a wave when the queue moves. They didn't and when I woke up and tried to get into the queue where I was, I was told in no uncertain terms to go. So I went up to the dunes, dug myself a small shallow trench and fell asleep until daybreak under the blanket I had.'

Gunner Geoffrey Parker, 225 Battery

'We made our way down to the beaches and lined up with the chaps. In the morning we had a look round to see if we could find a boat, but with no luck. We joined a queue in the sea up to our waists in water to get to a boat, but a Sergeant Major of the Engineers noticed we were gunners from the flash on our helmets and threatened to shoot us if we didn't leave. After that we split up.'

Trumpeter Stan Slade, 226 Battery

'We walked to Bray Dunes and stayed on the beaches until we decided to go into the water. We made a chain, but it got broken. We were picked up by the Margate lifeboat. I hung on to a rope on the side until I got aboard and Bert Stone also got on all right. I grabbed [Fred] Tugwell and got him on board as he couldn't swim a stroke. The lifeboat took us out to a ship anchored off the beaches and we had to climb up ropes to get onto it.'

Gunner George Tompkinson, 228 Battery

'I spent my 21st Birthday, the 30 May, on the beach at Dunkirk. We were told to help build a jetty out to the boats using three tonner lorries if we wanted to get out alive. [To make the improvised jetties, lorries were driven out as far as possible at low tide, linked together and planks used to cover the gaps]. I got away the next day on the gunboat H.M.S. Mosquito and they gave us a cup of tea for which we were very grateful. I later found out that the boat was sunk on the return journey to Dunkirk.'

Gunner Robert Ford, 227 Battery

'The truck gave out and with the petrol shortage we ended up walking until we got to Dunkirk. We had a nose round, then got onto the beach and that was pretty horrible. I got on a small boat, but so many men were trying to swim out to the ships, they got hold of the side and tipped it over. I looked at the ships and looked at the shore and went back to the shore which was closer.'

Gunner Edward McMahon, 227 Battery

'What remained of my troop and some from battery headquarters walked to Bray Dunes and we got a lot of the men away with an officer calling for Royal Artillery. They got us into packets as best as they could, but as soon as the Stukas came over, about every three hours, everyone scattered. You ran where you could and got under cover where you could. I was on the sands for three days and came off more or less on my own in the end. I had to swim nearly a quarter of a mile to a naval vessel. All I had on were my trousers and shirt and my revolver and soon as I got over the top from the nets, a Petty Officer took my revolver.'

Troop Sergeant Major George Coldman, 227 Battery

'I got to Dunkirk on the night of 30 May and it was burning, in fact the whole town seemed ablaze. I got in a wagon for a sleep and woke up to find the driver dead with a bullet wound. After two nights of bombing and machine gunning, some one was hit every time and if you missed them you were lucky. A Scotch chap and myself went down along the dunes, met a Major and found a rowing boat with oars, but it had a hole in it. So we got it on the water and the Major rowed like hell while we baled out the water with our tin hats. We got over to a fishing boat, went up the sides on ropes and then went below and stripped off, because we were soaking wet. We were then told to get dressed and got anybody's clothes but our own. We had to go on deck and were transferred over the top to the destroyer H.M.S. Vivacious - all this while the bombing was going on - but we got away and arrived safely at Folkestone.'

Gunner Don Booker, 228 Battery

'We finally got to Dunkirk. I thought look at this, what a mess, we will never make it and are going to be taken prisoner. So Bertie Ware and I went back into the town, I think it was La Panne and spoke to some of the lads who were about to hold the place for as long as they could. We were looking for a boat, but couldn't find one as everyone had the same idea. We were just about to give up when we saw a little shed. Bertie kicked the door open and there was a lovely little rowing boat. We asked three or four of the other guys walking about to give us a hand to get it into the water… and when we got there it sank! By this time, there were very few people left on the beach, most of the boats had gone and the rumours started that they were not coming back. So we took to the water. All we had was half a life jacket, but Bertie couldn't swim, so we got hold of something floating about and swam out pushing him along. We got to a small boat, but I can't remember who picked me up or even how I got out the water. When I woke up, a sailor said, drink that lad to Bertie and me. I will always remember it, because he had covered us in the coloured swathe used by the stokers. All I had on was a pair of breeches.'

Gunner William 'Jock' Giles, 226 Battery

Some of the men who had made unsuccessful attempts to get off the beaches went inland to look for food and water. In the cellars of Malo-les-Bains and Dunkirk they also found a brief respite from the bombing and shelling. The majority of these men would eventually make their escape from the mole which increasingly became the vital means of evacuation as the bridgehead contracted and the eastern end of the beaches were abandoned.

'When we arrived in Dunkirk, there were no boats just columns of men. We were formed into groups of 50, but then told that we were not going to get off that night and were to go into town, find a billet and kip down. We slept in a barbers' basement and used the shop in the morning to wash and shave. We came back onto the beach and finally ran the gauntlet on the mole, which had been damaged and had planks over it, and boarded a packed destroyer. A naval chap stood on the front of the mole directing everybody and even though there were still shells flying over he could have been standing on the street corner directing traffic.'

Gunner Bob Page, 227 Battery

'I arrived on the beaches and met Gunner Joe Forster and we laid down and went to sleep. Next morning I walked around the dock and found many abandoned vehicles full of stores and food. I collected a sandbag of food and a new battledress. I managed to wash and shave in an empty cafe and saw Sergeant Stone and other members of his troop. Going back to the beach we just sat around and waited, watching the long queues and dodging the bombs. We eventually got to the mole where a red-tabbed officer threatened to shoot anyone who did not sit down and wait his turn. Joe Forster and I eventually clambered on to a destroyer and arrived at Dover during the night.'

Gunner Ken Leake, 228 Battery

'I made my way back [from the beaches] where I met the Battery Commander, Major Christopher, who told me to go into a big house and wake up all the men in there and take them to a deserted restaurant and stay in the cellar. Here we also met some of our chaps from another battery. We couldn't get any water to drink, but managed to have a shave and had some tinned vegetables. Major Christopher arranged to get us into batches of 50 and put chalk numbers on our helmets. When our time came to run along the causeway to get on a ship out, a shell landed in front of us and we dived for cover over the side, but the sailor standing on the causeway shouted out to us to get up and run for the ship. We had to jump on and with the dive bombers overhead, the ship seemed to come out of the water and crash down. The guns were right in front of us firing on the ship and I was rather deaf for some time after. Anyway I found a spot to squeeze in on this ship. Despite the noise of the guns and the bombs and with the ship making its way to England, I fell asleep.'

Trumpeter Stan Slade, 226 Battery

‘At Dunkirk we were moved about a lot on the beach, joining one queue and then another. Eventually our group were detailed to move to the mole. We went along the mole, which had been badly damaged, walking or running along wooden planks in places until we came to a destroyer alongside. It was well below the level of the mole and we were jumping down on to the decks and sailors were grabbing us as we landed. As I jumped, aircraft came over and the ship’s company were called to action stations. I was in mid-air with no sailor to catch me. I hit the deck and slid along until I hit something that stopped me, but I turned my foot over which became very painful. On stand-down the sailors picked me up and took me down to the sick bay. It was thought only to be a sprained ankle, but they tied a label on me and gave me some lovely bread.’

Gunner Ken Johnson, 227 Battery

‘We more or less dug ourselves into the sand and had this old bedding wrapped round us. The Germans used to come over bombing and strafing, but you had no hope of hitting them with a rifle. While we were in this hole in the sand, an officer came up and asked what unit we were with. We said the 57th Anti-Tank, but where they are we don’t know as they are all scattered. So he said that he was getting parties up onto the mole and we would get onto a boat at night. They were still shelling like hell, so you ran so far, heard the shells coming over, then got down a bit, and in the end we got on this old steamboat. I thought it was like coming out of hell into heaven. In the big lounge in this steamboat, the three of us plonked ourselves down on this settee. I thought we would probably go further down the coast and start again from there, but of course they whipped us across to England. We were that tired when we got on the boat that we just went straight to sleep. We woke up when we heard them saying, ‘it’s Dover, it’s Dover’.

Gunner Jim Hills, 227 Battery

Getting on board a boat didn't necessarily guarantee a safe trip home, as Gunner Dennis Spink of 227 Battery described: 'We gradually moved along the mole. It had been hit a couple of times and there was some planking to negotiate. Finally we arrived at the end and boarded a destroyer. We were greeted by a cheerful matelot and settled down by the aft torpedo tubes as if we were already in England. The destroyer was quite loaded and we put out to sea, but after about 10 minutes some Stukas came over. We watched them quite casually until they dived on us, the light AA opened up but to no effect and a bomb dropped either side of us. It was only then that we realised it was becoming dangerous, Tommy Hyland dived under a torpedo tube together with a lot of others and I wormed my way on top of them looking up at the Stukas between the torpedoes. I saw one bomb coming straight for us, but it seemed so abstract as if we were quite safe, until the bomb exploded below decks and then another one hit forward. The destroyer immediately started listing and lots of wounded were screaming. I scrambled out, saw Tommy was hit and pulled him out. There was quite a lot of blood, but I thought it was only from his neck. I put both our field dressings around his neck and then another destroyer pulled alongside and someone shouted to put the wounded aboard. Together with a matelot I got Tommy over the side and they pulled me aboard as well. We went below deck and about one hour later were told that anyone not wounded was to go on deck. I went up, got over the side onto an old fishing boat with a big hold. After spending some time in the hold, I got back up on deck and we were told to jettison everything, including the [2-pounder] firing mechanism, tin hat, etc. We landed at Dover next day, I think it was the 1 June.'

By this date the danger of the military and naval situation was increasing hourly and the operation had reached its zenith in terms of the daily numbers embarked. The enemy guns were now in range of the harbour and only I Corps remained holding the British sector of the contracted defensive perimeter. To avoid the continued heavy loss in shipping, the evacuation was confined to the hours of darkness and it was expected to be completed during the coming night. It was not until late on Sunday 2 June, however, that the last of the British rearguard got away and the welcome signal was sent 'BEF evacuated'. The ships did return again on the following night to take off the French troops who had continued to fight on, but inevitably some remained. As the last ship left the Germans were already in the southern outskirts of Dunkirk itself and the formal surrender was made at 9 a.m. on the 4th. Later in the day the Admiralty announced that Operation Dynamo was officially ended.

NOTES

(1) Small, squat-looking ships, with their diesel engines astern and living quarters next to the engines, large numbers of these schuits had come over to Britain after the fall of Holland. Over forty were employed in the evacuation and the Horst was the only one lost, when on the last night it ran aground in the shallows off the West Mole and had to be abandoned.

(2) Due to poor communications between Dunkirk and Dover, the latter were unable to clarify a corrupt message that the harbour was blocked and as a result all ships were ordered to collect troops from the beaches. A good opportunity was missed as it was estimated that about 10,000 troops could have been lifted from the harbour during the night.

CHAPTER 10

Back Home

The Regimental Headquarters party under Lieutenant-Colonel Travers disembarked from the SS Horst at Margate at about 3 p.m. on Wednesday 29 May. After reluctantly handing over their rifles at the quay, they were taken in buses to the railway station, given mugs of tea and sandwiches, and then boarded a train that quickly departed. Its destination was unknown, but before midnight they arrived at the Infantry Training Centre (ITC) barracks at Devizes in Wiltshire, where everyone was fed, bathed and left to sleep. The next morning Regimental Headquarters was established in a hut adjacent to the ITC offices.

Their experience was typical of the troops returning from Dunkirk who were dealt with by an improvised but effective organisation to receive them. It was deemed necessary that no delay of any kind could be allowed at the ports and the men were put in waiting trains that drew out as soon as they were full. The loaded trains were then directed to chosen regulating stations where they received subsequent route and destination instructions. Reception areas were selected where home service troops were already stationed and who would look after the welfare of the returning men. It had also been foreseen that units would arrive in scattered parties, with little or no knowledge of the whereabouts of others of the same unit, and any re-organisation would have to take place afterwards.

The men came home tired, hungry, dishevelled, bereft of all their equipment, and unbelieving at the disaster that had overtaken the BEF. The relief of being safe at last competed with a sense of defeat and apprehension about the reception they would receive. Any fears were soon dispelled by the tremendous welcome they received from a civilian population relieved that so many of its men had escaped. Field service postcards were distributed at the railway stations to allow each man to let his family know that he was safe, while some threw notes out of the windows in the hope they would be forwarded.

As the trains passed through Surrey, or even halted at local stations, the men of the Regiment thought they might be going home only to be whisked down disappointedly to the West Country or farther afield. The temptation was too great for a small number, who made their way home only to face the desperate enquiries from mothers, wives and sweethearts for news of loved ones, some of whom were missing or had been killed. Eventually everyone would be sent home on a short leave.

With the imminent threat of invasion now hanging over the country, there was little time to relax and the re-organisation of the army got underway as quickly as possible. The area arranged for 44th Division was at Oxford, where Lieutenant-Colonel Travers and Captain Robinson arrived on 4 June to reform the Regiment. A camp was formed at Headington Hill Hall where officers and men arrived daily from various camps across the country.

On 8 June the Regiment moved to Port Meadow Camp, to the north and west of Oxford and on the River Isis as this stretch of the Thames is known. The men settled in under canvas and lacking any equipment, infantry training commenced. Two days later a solitary 2-pounder arrived from the workshops where it had been undergoing repairs since before the unit had gone overseas. The weather was warm and sunny and swimming in the river was popular. It all seemed a world away from the bombing and shelling of the previous weeks.

The camp was a place for many happy reunions, but they were tempered by the realisation of just how many faces were missing. The task of compiling records of those who had become casualties proved extremely difficult and it would be many months before the fate of the men posted as missing was confirmed, but the hope was that they would turn-up as prisoners of war.

An outline history of the Regiment published in Italy at the end of the war stated that seven officers and about 160 men had become casualties.(1) The records of the Commonwealth War Graves

Commission provide the names of three officers and 44 men who gave their lives and it is believed that a similar number were wounded, but returned home. Over 60 were taken as prisoners of war, with many wounded and all facing an indeterminate time in captivity. The losses in 226 Battery were the heaviest as it returned with barely over a quarter of its strength.

Across the channel, France had been forced to sign an armistice with Germany on 22 June and by this time Italy had also declared war on the allies. The map of Europe had changed dramatically since the outbreak of the war, but Britain with the support of the Commonwealth resolved to fight on, buoyed by the safe return of the bulk of its army and confident in the strength of its navy and airforce.

The Regiment remained at Port Meadow Camp until the end of the month, when it moved to Yorkshire, first to Pontefract and then the Doncaster area, to begin re-equipping and undertake its part in the defence of the country. It would also fight again in the deserts of North Africa and in the mountains of Italy. This story will be told in the next volume.

NOTES

(1) The officer casualties were Second-Lieutenant M.A. Edwards, Second-Lieutenant R.W. Smith-Stafford and Second-Lieutenant P.J. Dagleas (not confirmed until January 1941); Captain V.R.D. Hellaby, Lieutenant R. Wealleans and Second-Lieutenant G. Douglas were taken prisoner; and Second-Lieutenant R.G. Orr was wounded

APPENDICES

Appendix A ~ Roll of Honour

Allen, Percy J.	TSM	6141286	225 Battery
Commemorated on Dunkirk Memorial, France		31 May	Age 23
Askey, George	Gunner	3906041	228 Battery
Commemorated on Dunkirk Memorial, France		31 May - 2 June	Age 36
Atkinson, James	Gunner	1469691	226 Battery
Buried Longuenesse Souvenir Cemetery, France		29 May	Age 20
Ballard, Douglas B.	Gunner	6142965	226 Battery
Buried St. Venant Communal Cemetery, France		27 May	Age 20
Barlow, William A.	Gunner	6142330	226 Battery
Commemorated on Dunkirk Memorial, France		30-31 May	Age 20
Blanchard, Edward A.	TSM	1444507	228 Battery
Commemorated on Dunkirk Memorial, France		31 May	Age 25
Bond, George I.	Gunner	1058158	226 Battery
Buried St. Venant Communal Cemetery, France		27-31 May	Age 34
Bosman, Henry	Bombardier	6141222	228 Battery
Commemorated on Dunkirk Memorial, France		24 May	Age 21
Camp, Frederick J.	Bombardier	5618087	226 Battery
Buried Dunkirk Town Cemetery, France		25 May	Age 25
Catton, Thomas W.	Gunner	886464	225 Battery
Commemorated on Dunkirk Memorial, France		28 May	Age 19
Clarke, Leslie G.	Lance Bombardier	6142945	226 Battery
Commemorated on Dunkirk Memorial, France		27 May	Age 19
Cook, Robert G.	Gunner	4264616	226 Battery
Commemorated on Dunkirk Memorial, France		28 May	Age 33
Dagleas, Peter J.	2nd Lieutenant	88940	226 Battery
Buried Burbure Communal Cemetery, France		27 May	Age 26
Dixon, Robert W.	Gunner	1461685	226 Battery
Buried Eecke Churchyard, France		29 May - 2 June	Age 20
Dowling, Harry W.	Gunner	1476386	226 Battery
Buried St. Venant Communal Cemetery, France		25 May	Age 25
Edwards, Mervyn A. MC	2nd Lieutenant	73739	226 Battery
Buried Wormhoudt Communal Cemetery, France		25 May	Age 21

Evans, Harold V.	Lance Bombardier	1448719	226 Battery	
Commemorated on Dunkirk Memorial, France		29 May		Age 33
Featherstone, John R.	Gunner	842039	226 Battery	
Commemorated on Dunkirk Memorial, France		29 May - 2 June		Age 26
Gainey, Fred R.	Gunner	6140541	226 Battery	
Buried Longuenesse Souvenir Cemetery, France		29 May		Age 24
Gardner, Joseph A.	Lance Bombardier	828429	226 Battery	
Buried St. Sylvestre-Cappel New Cemetery, France		27-29 May		Age 26
Grandfield, Reginald T.	Gunner	6142043	226 Battery	
Buried Longuenesse Souvenir Cemetery, France		27 May - 2 June		Age 20
Hanley, Thomas F.	Lance Bombardier	6142410	226 Battery	
Commemorated on Dunkirk Memorial, France		29 May - 2 June		Age 22
Hayter, Percy R.	Gunner	1514712	226 Battery	
Buried Mechelen Communal Cemetery, Belgium		12 July		Age 21
Huxley, Arthur	Gunner	884070	226 Battery	
Buried Caestre Communal Cemetery, France		29 May		Age 20
Jaye, Leonard A.	Gunner	1524807	226 Battery	
Commemorated on Dunkirk Memorial, France		26 May		Age 20
Kirlew, Donald	Gunner	1514824	226 Battery	
Commemorated on Dunkirk Memorial, France		29 May		Age 21
Lake, William C.J.	Gunner	1450167	227 Battery	
Buried Le Grand Hasard Military Cemetery, France		25 May		Age 20
Langford, Thomas I.	Gunner	1469905	225 Battery	
Buried Helfaut Churchyard, France		4 June		Age 28
Long, Charles H.	Gunner	6142305	228 Battery	
Commemorated on Dunkirk Memorial, France		29 May		Age 18
Messenger, Walter H.	Gunner	1491432	225 Battery	
Commemorated on Dunkirk Memorial, France		26-28 May		Age 21
Oldham, George S.	Lance Bombardier	812898	226 Battery	
Buried St. Venant Communal Cemetery, France		12-31 May		Age 29
Poplett, James W. C.	Gunner	6135624	226 Battery	
Buried Longuenesse Souvenir Cemetery, France		29-31 May		Age 35
Purvis, G.	Gunner	777757	228 Battery	
Buried Esquelmes War Cemetery, Belgium.		22 May		Age 29

Ratledge, Jack M.	Gunner	1448179	226 Battery
Buried Eecke Churchyard, France		29 May - 2 June	Age 23
Reaney, Douglas	Sergeant	2043590	227 Battery
Buried Kaster Churchyard, Belgium		20 May	Age 19
Ring, Frank	Sergeant	6134459	227 Battery
Commemorated on Dunkirk Memorial, France		19 May	Age 37
Rivers, Frederic G.	Gunner	6141789	226 Battery
Buried St. Venant Communal Cemetery, France		30-31 May	Age 23
Robinson, John W.	Gunner	1457296	228 Battery
Buried Esquelmes War Cemetery, Belgium.		22-23 May	Age 20
Sellen, Edwin F.J.	Bombardier	6141790	226 Battery
Buried Cite Bonjean Military Cemetery, France		13 May	Age 22
Smith-Stafford, Ronald W.	2nd Lieutenant	109162	227 Battery
Commemorated on Dunkirk Memorial, France		24 May	
Snelling, George E.	Gunner	6142550	228 Battery
Buried Le Grand Hasard Military Cemetery, France		24 May	Age 18
Sutton, Mark	Gunner	1060315	225 Battery
Buried Le Grand Hasard Military Cemetery, France		27 May	Age 32
Vaughan, Louis D.	Gunner	6135508	228 Battery
Buried Marquise Communal Cemetery, France		31 May	Age 35
Walters, Norman H.	Lance Bombardier	1451778	226 Battery
Commemorated on Dunkirk Memorial, France		29 May	Age 20
Watson, James H.	Gunner	847008	226 Battery
Buried Caestre Communal Cemetery, France		29 May	Age 23
Woodhouse, Ralph J.E.	Gunner	1514727	226 Battery
Commemorated on Dunkirk Memorial, France		28 May	Age 20
Yorke, Alfred E.	Gunner	6142339	226 Battery
Buried Longuenesse Souvenir Cemetery, France		29 May	Age 19

Appendix B ~ Honours and Awards

Distinguished Service Order ~ Major J.R.C. Christopher
London Gazette 11 July 1940

This officer has shown outstanding courage, initiative, and fighting spirit throughout this period. I consider his Battery has accounted for the destruction of more enemy tanks than any other Battery under my command.

At present the losses in his Battery, of personnel alone, has amounted to 3 Officers and 82 O.Rs., out of 5 Officers and 118 O.Rs.

His excellent example has had the effect of keeping the morale of his Battery to its present high order and inflicting major casualties on the enemy.

Between May 27 and 30, at Caestre, when Major Christopher had only 3 guns remaining out of 12, they were so sited and efficiently controlled that 5 enemy tanks, in this area, were completely destroyed, and their crews remaining alive were all taken prisoners.

Major Christopher's Battery at this time was operating in close liaison with the 4th Battalion Royal Sussex Regiment, and I am of the opinion that by his action in the subsequent withdrawal, this Infantry Battalion was able to get away when nearly surrounded. The whole of the R.A.P. belonging to the 4th Royal Sussex at Caestre, consisting of 9 wounded men were evacuated by this officer's Battery.

He had the greatest difficulty in the withdrawal of his Battery to the Poperinghe area, under constant bombing, shell and small arms fire, and was (sic) the last British troops to leave Caestre.

Military Cross ~ Second-Lieutenant M.A. Edwards
London Gazette 22 October 1940

On 22 May 1940, one of the guns of this officer's Troop was in position north of the village of Petegem. This position was under heavy shell fire for three quarters of an hour and Second-Lieutenant Edwards, with great difficulty, reached his gun, where he instilled courage and calmness into the whole of the detachment.

He was ordered to withdraw his gun, and by his skilful handling was able to get it hooked on to his truck and out of action without any casualties.

Undoubtedly the lives of his detachment were saved by his cool-headedness and complete disregard of his own safety in a most difficult situation.

Military Cross ~ Captain P.G. Hampton
London Gazette 20 December 1940

In the operations in the vicinity of Aire - Morbecque, May 22-25. Captain Hampton showed exceptional initiative and boldness in handling his anti-tank guns in the face of hostile tank attack. In spite of having two guns destroyed by enemy fire, he brought a further gun into action to cover his exposed flank, thus limiting the action of the hostile tanks between Morbecque and Hazebrouck.

Military Cross ~ Lieutenant G. Douglas
London Gazette 25 September 1947

On the 22 May 1940, Lieutenant Gordon Douglas, 57 Anti-Tank Regiment, Royal Artillery, was commanding a section of two 2-pounder anti-tank guns, the role of which was to deny the rapidly advancing enemy the crossing of the Petegemstraat - Langestraat road (in the vicinity of Oudenarde) and thus cover the position of the 5th Battalion The Royal Sussex Regiment. Heavy dive-bombing destroyed one of the guns of the section, killing the detachment (less one man).

Lieutenant Douglas continued for two hours to hold his position with the remaining gun and two Bren guns. It was attacked three times by the enemy infantry. The first two attacks were broken up by his determined resistance. In the third heavy attack his position was entirely surrounded, but for two hours he held on until almost every round of small arms ammunition was expended and the enemy infantry had closed in. He then fired off all the remaining anti-tank shells and (having no lanyard) showed great coolness in destroying his own gun by putting a round down the muzzle and firing the gun by kicking the emergency firing lever; in doing so he was wounded in the face and chest.

Throughout the whole action Lieutenant Douglas displayed the greatest coolness and devotion to duty.

Military Cross ~ Second-Lieutenant R.G. Orr
London Gazette 20 December 1940

On May 26, during a reconnaissance in the Bois de Huit Rues, it was reported to Lieutenant Orr that an enemy tank had been seen at the south-west corner of the wood.

As it was impossible, owing to the trees, to get his 2-pounder gun into a suitable position, Lieutenant Orr armed himself with an anti-tank rifle, which he obtained from the infantry.

Then, together with two other officers, he manoeuvred to a favourable position, from which he could engage this tank. The tank was in a 'hide-out', and eight rounds were fired at it by Lieutenant Orr, five being direct hits. The tank was put out of action.

The officer, throughout, displayed great courage, coolness and initiative in the command of his troop, and his example to the men under his command has been magnificent. During the period under review Second-Lieutenant Orr's troop destroyed five enemy tanks.

Military Medal ~ Lance Bombardier E. Stredwick
London Gazette 20 December 1940

This Lance Bombardier was one of a gun detachment of six men belonging to J Troop. During the action at Morbecque on 24 May 1940, this gun was ordered into an emergency position just off the main road leading into Hazebrouck. On arrival eight enemy tanks approached at a distance of 1,000 yards. The leading tank was at once put out of action, and the detachment came under heavy shell and small arms fire from the remaining tanks. A second tank was then hit and also put out of action. One enemy tank was able to manoeuvre in rear of the gun position and this tank was engaged and put out of action.

By the gallantry and devotion to duty of this gun detachment the enemy tanks were diverted and a critical situation was saved.

Military Medal ~ Gunner W. H. Messenger
London Gazette 11 July 1940

On 27 May 1940 this man was No 3 of a gun sited at the south-west corner of the Forêt de Nieppe. A large column of enemy infantry were seen advancing towards his gun position, flanked by machine guns.

Fire was opened on his gun position from about 200 yards range, and Gunner Messenger was immediately wounded in the hand and leg. In spite of his wounds he remained at his gun, and continued firing at the advancing enemy. This had the effect of temporarily silencing the enemy's machine guns, and held up their advance.

When nearly surrounded and forced out of their gun position, Gunner Messenger together with the whole of his gun crew, withdrew to their vehicles and got away safely.

Military Medal ~ Lance Bombardier C.W. Dunn
London Gazette 25 September 1947

On 22 May 1940 Lance Bombardier Dunn, 228 Battery, 57 Anti-Tank Regiment R.A. displayed outstanding gallantry and devotion to duty in supporting his Section Commander in face of overwhelming enemy attacks in the vicinity of Oudenarde.

The role of the Section was the denial to the enemy of the crossing of the Petegemstraat - Langestraat Road, thus covering the position of 5th Battalion The Royal Sussex Regiment.

Heavy dive-bombing had destroyed one of the guns, killing the detachment (less one man) but for two hours this N.C.O., with the greatest coolness and efficiency, supported the Section Commander in holding the position in face of three attacks by enemy infantry. The first two attacks were broken up by this determined resistance but the third completely surrounded the position.

For two hours, until ammunition was exhausted, the enemy was held at bay, when the Section Commander destroyed the remaining anti-tank gun, despite the previous loss of the lanyard, which resulted in his being wounded. To the last Lance Bombardier Dunn displayed the greatest coolness and devotion to duty in face of heavy odds and his outstanding gallantry was in keeping with the highest traditions of the Royal Regiment.

Military Medal ~ Signalman E. J. Bonsall
44th Divisional Signals, attached 57th Anti-Tank Regiment, R.A.
London Gazette 11 July 1940

This man was one of the three Dispatch Riders employed on my H.Q. On the evening of 22 May 1940 when the Regiment was withdrawing from its Battle positions this man displayed such tenacity of purpose and understanding in locating and co-ordinating the various troop movements that the whole operation was carried out with minimum casualties. These Dispatch Riders were subjected to heavy shelling and bombing, yet time after time they went out on their tasks cheerfully and willingly in spite of having been deprived of sleep the preceding night, and facing very real danger. Their work was outstanding and demanded a very high degree of personal courage.
(Recommended by Lieutenant-Colonel R.L. Travers)

2/Lieutenant M.A. Edwards
Military Cross

2/Lieutenant G. Douglas
Military Cross

2/Lieutenant R.G. Orr
Military Cross

Bombardier E. Stredwick
Military Medal

Appendix C ~ Roll of Officers and Other Ranks proceeding to France in April 1940

Regimental Headquarters

Travers R.L.	Lieut-Col	
Chapman G.P.	Major	
Foulger R.E.A.	Capt	
Rathbone C.P.H.	2/Lieut	
Peace H.C.	Lieut (QM)	
Whitelaw J.C.G.	Lieut (RAMC)	
Elwes J.C.	Lieut (RAOC)	
Donald G.B.	2/Lieut (RCS)	
Moore T.	A/RSM	1048008
Dannatt F.	RQMS	6135728
Adams A.	Gnr	6139360
Ashman A.	Gnr	6135602
Bailey W.	L/Sgt	6142013
Benbow A.	Gnr	794839
Booth F.	Gnr Mtr/Mch	1059218
Clark G.	Gnr	1497506
Clark T.	Gnr	828092
Cole S.	Gnr	818057
Crawshaw W.	W/Bdr	1453490
Dell R.	Gnr	777433
Driffill S.	Gnr	1445582
Elson A.	Dr (IC)	6142363
Feagan P.	Gnr	6141777
Fray P.	Gnr	6141296
Gainey E.	Dr (IC)	6142570
Gilbert A.	Dr (IC)	1462608
Gold R.	Gnr	1452932
Grove F.	Gnr	1462965
Halliwell R.	Dr (IC)	6142349
Harris J.	L/Bdr	6142557
Harwood F.	Gnr	6140377
Hinton N.	Dr (IC)	1448499
Johnson R.	Dr (IC)	1448736
Latter W.	Gnr	6141704
Maskell A.	Gnr	1425621
Moody E.	Dr (IC)	6138881
Parfitt L.	Gnr	826202
Parminter K.	Dr (IC)	1462946
Paul S.	Tpr	6142317
Perry J.	Gnr	6138265
Reynolds R.	Gnr	1472416
Roper F.	A/Sgt	1448176
Shepherd A.	Gnr	6141248
Steer H.	Gnr	1448443
Thorns A.	Dr (IC)	1462654
Wadey T.	Gnr	1451840
Watkins L.	Gnr	6142528
Wheeler G.	Dr (IC)	6140582
White L.	Dr (IC)	1456248
Woodall A.	Gnr	843494
Worrall S.	Dr (IC)	6142032
Young A	Gnr	6711665

225 Anti-Tank Battery

Robinson T.H.	Capt	
Mayberry R.G.	Capt	
Hutton E.R.	Lieut	
Orr R.G.	2/Lieut	
Clacher H.	BSM	1051020
Coddington J.	W/BSM	6136844
Allen P.	W/TSM	6141286
Holden F.	W/TSM	6197570
Blenkinsop J.	A/BQMS	1044473
Alexander P.	Gnr	822645
Alford T	Gnr	1491305
Andrew P.	Gnr Dr/Mch	6141258
Atkinson J.	Gnr	1069852
Ayre A.	Gnr	1059075
Baker F.	W/Bdr	6141504
Banister S.	Dr (IC)	6142034
Barker F.	Gnr	838192

Barnett D.	Gnr	1451721
Baxter E.	W/Sgt/Ftr	6140313
Baxter S.	L/Sgt	6142333
Beaton G.	Dr (IC)	6141746
Beer E.	Dr (IC)	1445104
Belton J.	Gnr Dr/Mch	6142035
Betts V.	Dr (IC)	6141765
Blackmore L.	Gnr	1491320
Blewitt F.	W/Bdr	2563581
Boon C.	Gnr	1452738
Boswell J.	Dr (IC)	1457170
Boyle F.	Gnr	4607443
Bradwell N.	L/Bdr	1055255
Bragginton A.	Dr (IC)	1447126
Breed A.	Dr (IC)	1441505
Brewer H.	Gnr	818677
Bruce R.	W/Bdr Mtr/Mch	6142363
Bucksey T.	Gnr	6141512
Burke N.	Gnr	884846
Callan J.	Dr (IC)	1464606
Callingham H.	L/Bdr	5491600
Campany R.	Gnr	806255
Carberry F.	L/Bdr	810594
Catton T.	Gnr	886464
Champlouvier A.	Gnr	6136640
Chubb G.	Gnr	1514771
Clensell F.	A/Bdr	815216
Collyer J.	Gnr	6140360
Corfield J.	Gnr	781399
Crofts D.	Dr (IC)	1448712
Crutchley E.	L/Bdr	5044840
Dash J.	Gnr	784625
Davies S.	Gnr	1445364
Dealler J.	A/Bdr	835439
Dean F.	Gnr	1050335
Desborough W.	L/Sgt	6142000
Fallon C.	Gnr	1439384
Gadsby W.	Gnr	6527937
Gillham S.	Gnr	1440256
Goodwill F.	Gnr	818152
Gorman R.	Dr (IC)	3244264
Gotsell J.	Gnr	1441868
Hanson D.	L/Bdr Mtr/Mch	828530
Harrington C.	A/Bdr	6142465
Harris F.	Gnr	4613779
Harvie H.	Gnr	1470002
Hayes N.	Gnr	6142980
Henderson R.	Dr (IC)	818631
Hendry H.	Dr (IC)	816853
Hickey J.	Gnr	1025073
Hinton T.	Gnr	6138908
Holmes L.	Gnr	6142901
Hubbard L.	Gnr	514818
Hughes H.	A/Bdr	1069321
Jessup R.	Gnr	648505
Johnson G.	Dr (IC)	868463
Kelley R.	Gnr	6141259
Keysell A.	Gnr	6142955
King A.	Gnr	6142946
Langford T.	Gnr	1469905
Long B.	Gnr	6138852
Large R.	Gnr	1514825
Lavender C.	Dr (IC)	1445902
Leary L.	A/Bdr	1448474
Leary T.	L/Bdr	1448744
Lockett W.	Gnr	6142985
Mason R.	Dr (IC)	1451665
McCabe B.	Dr (IC)	6527586
McCloud A.	Gnr	7013280
McCorkell R.	Gnr	1469545
Mead J.	Gnr	1451790
Messenger W.	Gnr	1491432
Minnitt F.	Gnr	1448637
Neville E.	Gnr	1443237
O'Riordan M.	Gnr	1491446
Olive S.	Gnr	1440547
Otton S.	Dr (IC)	1514773
Palfreeman H.	Gnr	1514832
Parker G.	Gnr	1450261
Paterson A.	L/Sgt	2217589
Peters W.	Gnr	6143005
Pryor R.	Gnr	1491462

Pyatt. R.	A/Bdr	6142400
Read R.	Gnr	1514699
Richardson S.	Gnr	1514841
Robinson D.	Dr (IC)	1469735
Rutter R.	Gnr	6142903
Saunders H.	Dr (IC)	6140564
Simmonds R.	W/Sgt	6136848
Slack T.	Gnr	3654410
Smith N.	Gnr	1448180
Smith R.	Dr (IC)	1441683
Spencer T.	Gnr	1514849
Spurgeon W.	Gnr	6142046
Stevens A.	Gnr	6142037
Stewart W.	Sgt	6906708
Stretton F.	W/Sgt	6138598
Stuttle G.	Gnr Mtr/Mch	833797
Sullivan H.	Gnr	1451089
Sutton M.	Gnr	1060315
Taylor H.	Gnr	842160
Tilley W.	Gnr	6142049
Wakeman S.	Gnr	1514869
Waldon A.	Gnr	6142947
Watson P	W/Sgt	779795
Weaver J.	Gnr	6142472
Webster J.	Gnr	840789
Weedon T.	Dr (IC)	1441893
Wileman A.	L/Bdr	6140295
Williams H.	Gnr	1146336
Wormald J.	Dr (IC)	2315605
Worrall W.	Dr (IC)	62313
Wurker W.	L/Sgt	1461182
Wyatt G.	Dr (IC)	1462075
Young A.	L/Sgt	6140719

226 Anti-Tank Battery

Christopher J.R.C.	Major	
Sears B.L.	Capt	
Wealleans R.	Lieut	
Dagleas P.J.	2/Lieut	
Edwards M.A.	2/Lieut	
Thomas G.	W/BSM	6137028
Rowland A.	A/TSM	6138980
Brown J.	W/BQMS	1445560

Adney E.	Gnr	1024257
Anstiss H.	Gnr	821694
Atkin J.	A/Bdr	797672
Atkinson J.	Gnr	1469691
Attfield G.	Gnr	1057280
Ballard D.	Gnr	6142965
Ballard V.	A/Sgt	6144763
Barlow W.A.	Gnr	6142330
Barlow W.S.	Gnr	874226
Blackman K.	A/Bdr	1450144
Blackwell W.	Gnr	1516664
Bodkin C.	Gnr	1516682
Bond G.	Gnr	1058158
Bone A.	Dr (IC)	6142379
Brown R.	Gnr	1073240
Burgess J.	Gnr	851319
Burrow M.	Dr (IC)	6142941
Camp F.	A/Bdr	5618087
Chandler C.	Gnr	6141748
Chick G.	Dr (IC)	1453485
Clarke L.	L/Bdr	6142945
Cloutt F.	L/Sgt	6140110
Cole H.	A/Bdr	6142381
Connor E.	Dr (IC)	1070783
Cook R.	Gnr	4264616
Crundwell W.	Gnr	6142331
Darbon J.	Gnr	6142938
Darbon J.W.	Dr (IC)	6141797
Davis M.	Gnr Dr/Mch	1454369
Dixon R.	Gnr	1461685
Doig H.	L/Sgt	6141509
Dowling H.	Dr (IC)	1476386
Evans H.	L/Bdr	1448719
Falconer G.	Dr (IC)	1459123
Featherstone J.	Dr (IC)	842039
Fieldhouse R.	Gnr	1514807
Finch J.	Gnr	840665

Forsythe C.	A/Sgt	792732
Fuller C.	A/Bdr	6142493
Gainey F.	Dr (IC)	6140541
Gardner J.	L/Bdr	828429
Gibson E.	Gnr	1073485
Giles W.	Gnr	6141772
Goldthorpe A.	Gnr	1439243
Grafton G.	Gnr	6141770
Grandfield R.	Dr (IC)	6142043
Greenhough E.	Gnr	1514811
Gregory F.	Gnr	2048012
Hall L.	Gnr	6143001
Hanley T.	L/Bdr	6142410
Harper R.	Gnr	6140079
Harris C.	A/Bdr	6140577
Harris S.	Dr (IC)	6143010
Hay R.	Gnr	6140375
Hayter P.	Gnr	1514712
Henson J.	Dr (IC)	6142962
Hewitt W.	Dr (IC)	1445989
Hill D.	Tpr	1476387
Hinton B.	Dr (IC)	6148414
Hooper I.	Gnr Dr/Mch	1451704
Howarth J.	Gnr	800698
Huxley A.	Gnr	884070
Jackman R.	Gnr	5619996
Jacques G.	Dr (IC)	1445733
Jay N.	Gnr	1476389
Jaye L.	Gnr	1524807
Jeffries G.	Gnr	1514705
Kirlew D.	Gnr	1514824
Lawrence J.	Gnr Dr/Mch	1439928
Leary S.	Dr (IC)	6142571
Mansell F.	Dr (IC)	1450136
Morgan F.	Gnr	885066
Mullins W.	A/Bdr	815334
Neild L.	Gnr	1057013
Neville S.	Sgt	6138601
O'Donnell D.	L/Sgt	1451821
O'Sullivan W.	L/Bdr	1450476
Oldham G.	L/Bdr	812898

Parry J.	Gnr	1450149
Parsons H.	Gnr	1514744
Poplett J.	Gnr	6135624
Proctor P.	Gnr	1514838
Pryse W.	W/Bdr	6141288
Ratledge J.	Gnr Dr/Mch	1448179
Reeves A.	Dr (IC)	6141787
Rivers F.	Dr (IC)	6141789
Roberts J.	A/Bdr	777180
Roberts J.	Gnr	1439251
Robinson E.	Dr (IC)	6142348
Robinson K.	A/Bdr	1448758
Robinson P.	L/Sgt	6140292
Roots L.	Gnr	6140566
Russell A.	Gnr	6141522
Sellen E.	A/Bdr	6141790
Sheppard G.	Gnr	6140548
Simms R.	Gnr	1426254
Slade S.	Tpr	6138956
Smith S.	Gnr	777491
Smithers W.	Gnr Dr/Mch	6142397
Southall J.	Gnr	886323
Spragg J.	Gnr	806739
Stedman J.	Sgt	7870637
Sterisbrick H.	Dr (IC)	1451769
Sykes E.	Gnr	1514862
Tavener V.	Gnr	6142917
Wadsworth P.	Gnr	806782
Walker E.	Gnr	6142095
Walters N.	L/Bdr	1451778
Ware H.	Dr (IC)	6141760
Watson J.	Dr (IC)	847008
Weir J.	Gnr	872501
Whittaker J.	Gnr	754811
Woodhouse R.	Gnr	1514727
Yalden H.	Gnr	6142338
Yorke A.	Gnr	6142339

227 Anti-Tank Battery

Abbott G.S.	Capt
Westwood N.C.	Capt

Davis G.W.	Lieut	
Smith-Stafford R.W.	2/Lieut	
Twycross E.	A/BSM	779406
Coldman G.	W/TSM	6138838
Ross A.	A/TSM	6138586
Burrell W.	W/BQMS	6140259
Acott D.	A/Bdr	6141708
Allman F.	L/Bdr	818786
Baker W.	L/Sgt	6141551
Bangs R.	A/Bdr	6140279
Bates A.	Gnr	2081174
Bedwell T.	W/Bdr	6140789
Beresford C.	Gnr	1514789
Bewsher R.	A/Bdr	1443800
Blake G.	Gnr	1063985
Bowles W.	W/Bdr	1452736
Boxall J.	Gnr	1452737
Bozzard S.	Gnr	1066114
Bridger E.	Gnr	1064076
Brooker J.	Gnr	1441511
Browne K.	Gnr	1448705
Bryne W.	Gnr	1061617
Bunge J.	L/Bdr	6142970
Care J.	Gnr	802884
Carter T.	Gnr	1491335
Chadwick A.	Gnr	1066392
Chalker W.	L/Bdr	1046322
Chew N.	Gnr	5050004
Childs G.	A/Bdr	6140512
Coates J.	Gnr	4271787
Cocks H.	Dr (IC)	1442817
Cooper E.	Gnr	7245205
Cope F.	Dr (IC)	824730
Copestake D.	Gnr	808354
Cornish J.	Dr (IC)	6140096
Courtney J.	Gnr	1445905
Dalton W.	L/Bdr	822470
Dowd D.	L/Bdr	822816
Duke L.	Gnr	6140751
Dyer D.	Dr (IC)	2061693
Ebbett E.	Gnr	6142370
Elliott J.	Gnr	1491361
Evans G.	Dr (IC)	1440473
Feltham G.	Gnr	6141246
Flye R.	Gnr	1073641
Ford R.	Dr (IC)	6142378
Ford R.	Gnr	2061905
Gale A.	Gnr	1442825
Gane P.	Gnr	1448642
Goble R.	Gnr	1436895
Greene A.	Gnr Dr/Mch	1448646
Harper J.	L/Bdr	1032545
Harper P.	Gnr	1452693
Harris A.	Dr (IC)	1454251
Hartlebury E.	Gnr	6142335
Hartnett W.	L/Sgt	6143006
Higginson W.	Gnr	6140748
Hills J.	Gnr	2060634
Hodge R.	Gnr	5613836
Hodge T.	Gnr	6138954
Homden W.	Gnr	794260
Hughes A.	Dr (IC)	6142409
Humphreys W.	Gnr	1514810
Hurtley J.	Gnr	1439248
Hyland T.	Gnr	1439887
Ingham G.	Gnr	1514820
Iris C.	Gnr	1026971
Johnson J.	Gnr	6454590
Johnson K.	Gnr Dr/Mch	1452937
Kehoe A.	Dr (IC)	1450431
Lake W.	Gnr	1450167
Lawes A.	Dr (IC)	853548
Lawrence W.	Dr (IC)	6141261
Lloyd-Ellis C.	Dr (IC)	1450131
Mainwaring W.	Gnr	3958390
McCulloch H.	L/Bdr	1450904
McKeever J.	Gnr	1438703
McMahon E.	Gnr	6142440
Morrison J.	Gnr	1514830
Mould F.	Dr (IC)	6142479

Murdock R.	L/Bdr	797793
Myers G.	L/Sgt	6141795
Naylor L.	Dr (IC)	1437552
Nightingale D.	Dr (IC)	6141520
Nunes B.	Gnr	1514629
Paice F.	Gnr Dr/Mch	1452928
Packer G.	Gnr	6141508
Page R.	Gnr	6142480
Parkhouse R.	Dr (IC)	1452929
Parsons W.	Gnr	781571
Patterson J.	Gnr	1491458
Paxton D.	Gnr	1051619
Payne A.	Gnr	1066059
Perry S.	Gnr	1514611
Quirk R.	Gnr	1514633
Reaney D.	A/Sgt	2043590
Reed R.	Gnr	6140407
Reffell J.	Gnr Dr/Mch	1454229
Ring F.	Sgt	6134459
Rowland J.	Dr (IC)	6141502
Rowland W.	Gnr	6141505
Rowley E.	Gnr	1514678
Rowley L.	Dr (IC)	6142512
Salmon A.	Gnr	5498372
Sanders T.	Dr (IC)	1453727
Savage G.	Gnr	1448625
Selley S.	Gnr	6142422
Smart G.	Gnr	6143017
Smith C.	Gnr	1039713
Smith N.	A/Sgt	1452914
Smith R.	Gnr	6138272
Smith V.	W/Sgt	1870797
Spink D.	Gnr	2060789
Stephens P.	Gnr	1458512
Stokes R.	Gnr	1452569
Stone G.	Gnr	6140736
Storey A.	Dr (IC)	4271047
Strafford R.	Gnr	1514859
Taylor F.	Gnr	1514653
Tennent T.	Dr (IC)	1491505
Throp H.	Gnr	1514640
Tizzard A.	Gnr	6142336
Turner A.	Dr (IC)	1462931
Tyrell J.	Gnr	6142793
Vidler R.	L/Bdr	6527819
Vincent J.	A/Sgt	2045711
Warren F.	Gnr	5184512
Weller A.	Dr (IC)	2060787
West J.	Gnr Dr/Mch	6140778
Westmorland W.	Gnr	1514874
White E.	L/Sgt	1448621
Wolfe S.	Gnr	1514875
Woodhouse J.	Gnr	1456227
Wright L.	Gnr	1437557
Younghusband D.	Dr (IC)	1491535

228 Anti-Tank Battery

Hampton P.G.	Capt
Hellaby V.R.D.	Capt
Golding G.T.	Lieut
Douglas G.	2/Lieut
Goodman L.W.	2/Lieut

Briar H.	A/BSM	1066886
Blanchard E.	A/TSM	1444507
Gorton P.	BQMS	2605583

Akers S.	Dr (IC)	1462659
Alexander W.	Gnr Dr/Mch	6143007
Allsop W.	Gnr	781513
Askey G.	Gnr	3906041
Ayling A.	Gnr	6141264
Barnes A.	Dr (IC)	878545
Bartlett H.	A/Sgt	1450414
Bithell F.	Gnr	1065839
Boniface V.	Gnr	1462941
Booker A.	Gnr	1458284
Bosman H.	W/Bdr	6141222
Bourne G.	Dr (IC)	850191
Brisk J.	Gnr	1457300
Bruford C.	Gnr Dr/Mch	1462961
Budd J.	L/Sgt	1442297

Bullen V.	Gnr	6140731	Hughes J.	L/Bdr	6138670
Burfitt J.	Dr (IC)	1070378	Ielden D.	Dr (IC)	1462639
Campbell J.	Gnr	2756026	Jolley F.	Gnr	809439
Canham J.	L/Bdr	6142408	Kernot P.	Gnr	1439237
Casselden D.	W/Bdr	6142966	Lambert P.	Gnr	1444639
Cerasoli J.	Gnr	1514624	Lamberth F.	Gnr	1447174
Clark R.	Dr (IC)	6141526	Lamberth J.	Gnr	1441624
Complin W.	Dr (IC)	1073565	Langton J.	Gnr	6142934
Cooper W.	Gnr	802701	Leake K.	Gnr	1516633
Cornford J.	Gnr Dr/Mch	6140590	Levesconte R.	Gnr	5493828
Coulson S.	L/Bdr	1062083	Lewis G.	A/Bdr	1458501
Crossey R.	Gnr	840205	Long C.	Gnr	6142305
Crowe T.	Gnr	826850	Long R.	Dr (IC)	6140258
Crump C.	Gnr	1065648	Longworth E.	Dr (IC)	1498345
Dangerfield H.	A/Bdr	1071669	Lovett S.	A/Sgt	6840647
Darracott B.	Gnr	1063190	Marner T.	Bdr	727868
Dingwall W.	Gnr	2820712	Maynard A.	Gnr	6138855
Dunn C.	Gnr	798815	Mayne W.	Gnr	1442398
Ellis A.	Gnr	1439407	Morton S.	Dr (IC)	3246278
Espey J.	Gnr	842787	Munro D.	Dr (IC)	883755
Farrar E.	Dr (IC)	840908	Murman T.	A/Bdr	798305
Finch E.	Gnr Dr/Mch	1462939	Newman B.	Gnr	828839
Forster J.	Gnr	1454621	Newman M.	Gnr	1031571
Fraser R.	Gnr	6142981	Ostler O.	Gnr	1514765
Friday K.	Gnr	1448728	Owen W.	Gnr	824916
Geare M.	Dr (IC)	1462610	Parsons W.	Dr (IC)	1514735
Graham J.	Gnr	3595037	Phillips B.	Gnr	1450447
Greenfield A.	Gnr	6140361	Pillings C.	Dr (IC)	2058377
Greenfield F.	L/Sgt	6141752	Pratt H.	Gnr	1514753
Greensmith A.	Gnr	794009	Pritchard W.	Dr (IC)	1462653
Grover D.	Dr (IC)	1462955	Purvis G.	Gnr	777757
Hall J.	Gnr	1069417	Reed R.	Gnr	1514738
Hand C.	Gnr	1491396	Robinson J.	Dr (IC)	1457296
Hansford E.	Gnr	1514701	Rogers E.	Gnr	1491467
Harris R.	Gnr	840637	Rose G.	Gnr	1498933
Harris W.	Gnr	2054477	Rowe F.	Gnr	872755
Harrison W.	Gnr	1470022	Russ B.	Gnr	6142334
Hayes W.	Dr (IC)	790743	Russell R.	A/Sgt	6142462
Hicks S.	Gnr	6142048	Sancaster F.	Gnr	1435584
Hoare H.	Gnr	1455526	Sanders F.	Sgt	2206124
Howlett G.	Gnr	1514737	Sandland T.	Gnr	1439246

Scott C.	Gnr	6142933	Tindall S.	Gnr	1462618
Sewell S.	Dr (IC)	1458193	Tompkinson G.	Gnr	1456687
Sheard C.	Gnr	1439253	Tugwell F.	Tpr	6136075
Simmons A.	Gnr	1491494	Turner H.	Sgt	743026
Skilton F.	Gnr	6142447	Vaughan L.	Bdr	6135508
Smallbone K.	Tpr	6138669	Wakefield N.	Gnr	6143012
Smith H.	Gnr	1491496	Watts R.	Dr (IC)	1462965
Snelling G.	Gnr	6142550	Weeks W.	L/Bdr	6140714
Spark J.	Gnr	1462617	Williams A.	Dr (IC)	1448766
Steedon L.	Gnr	6527655	Wilson T.	W/Sgt	5823674
Stone A.	L/Sgt	1462917	Witkiss C.	Gnr	876344
Stredwick E.	L/Bdr	6141734	Worrall R.	Gnr	821002
Taylor H.	Gnr	884318	Wright R.	Gnr	1439240
Tetlow J.	Dr (IC)	1065705			
Thomson G.	Gnr	6142535			

Every effort has been made to verify the spelling and listing of names, ranks and army numbers in this roll, but some errors will no doubt have remained. The author will be pleased to be notified of any corrections.

Service numbers beginning 613.... and 614.... denote enlistment in The East Surrey Regiment.

Abbreviations

Gnr	Gunner	BSM	Battery Sergeant Major
Dr (IC)	Driver Internal Combustion (engine)	RQMS	Regimental Quartermaster Sergeant
Dr Mech	Driver Mechanic	RSM	Regimental Sergeant Major
Mtr/Mch	Motor Mechanic	QM	Quartermaster
Tpr	Trumpeter	2/Lieut	Second Lieutenant
Ftr	Fitter	Lieut	Lieutenant
L/Bdr	Lance Bombardier	Capt	Captain
Bdr	Bombardier	Major	
L/Sgt	Lance Sergeant	Lieut-Col	Lieutenant-Colonel
Sgt	Sergeant		
TSM	Troop Sergeant Major	A/...	Acting ...
BQMS	Battery Quartermaster Sergeant	W/ ...	War Substantive ...

Appendix D ~ Key Appointments, May 1940

Regimental Headquarters
Lieutenant-Colonel R.L. Travers, OBE .... Commanding Officer
Major G.P. Chapman, DSO, MC .... Second-in-Command
Captain R.E.A. Foulger .... Adjutant
2/Lieutenant C.P.H. Rathbone .... Liaison Officer

Lieutenant (QM) H.C. Peace .... Quartermaster
RSM T. Moore
RQMS F. Dannatt

Lieutenant J.C.G. Whitelaw (RAMC) .... Medical Officer
Lieutenant J.C. Elwes (RAOC) .... Ordnance Mech. Engineer
2/Lieutenant G.B. Donald (RCS) .... Signals Officer

225 Battery
Captain T.H. Robinson .... Battery Commander
Captain R.G. Mayberry .... Battery Captain
Lieutenant E.R. Hutton .... Reconnaissance Officer

2/Lieutenant R.G. Orr .... Troop Commander
TSM P. Allen .... Troop Commander
TSM F. Holden .... Troop Commander

BSM H. Clacher
BQMS J. Blenkinsop

226 Battery
Major J.R.C. Christopher .... Battery Commander
Captain B.L. Sears .... Battery Captain
Lieutenant R. Wealleans .... Reconnaissance Officer

2/Lieutenant P.J. Dagleas .... Troop Commander
2/Lieutenant M.A. Edwards .... Troop Commander (E)
TSM A. Rowland .... Troop Commander

BSM G. Thomas
BQMS J. Brown

227 Battery

Captain G.S. Abbott .... Battery Commander
Captain N.C. Westwood .... Battery Captain
Lieutenant G.W. Davis .... Reconnaissance Officer

2/Lieutenant R.W. Smith-Stafford .... Troop Commander (G)
TSM A.G. Ross .... Troop Commander (H)
TSM G. Coldman .... Troop Commander (I)

BSM E.Twycross
BQMS W. Burrell

228 Battery

Captain P.G. Hampton .... Battery Commander
Captain V.R.D. Hellaby .... Battery Captain
Lieutenant G.T. Golding .... Reconnaissance Officer

TSM E. Blanchard .... Troop Commander (J)
2/Lieutenant G. Douglas .... Troop Commander (K)
2/Lieutenant L.W. Goodman .... Troop Commander (L)

BSM H. Briar
BQMS P. Gorton

(From 15 May Captain T.H. Robinson appointed Adjutant and Captain R.E.A. Foulger commanding 225 Battery)

Lieutenant-Colonel R.L. Travers OBE
Commanding Officer

Major G.P. Chapman DSO MC
Second-in-Command

Captain R.E.A. Foulger
Adjutant

Captain T.H. Robinson
225 Battery

Major J.R.C. Christopher
226 Battery

Captain G.S. Abbott
227 Battery

Captain P.G. Hampton
228 Battery

Appendix E ~ Order of Battle

44th (Home Counties) Infantry Division – May 1940
Major-General E.A. Osborne

131st Infantry Brigade Brigadier J.E. Utterson-Kelso
2nd Battalion The Buffs
1/5th Battalion The Queen's Royal Regiment
1/6th Battalion The Queen's Royal Regiment

132nd Infantry Brigade Brigadier J.S. Steele
1st Battalion The Queen's Own Royal West Kent Regiment
4th Battalion The Queen's Own Royal West Kent Regiment
5th Battalion The Queen's Own Royal West Kent Regiment

133rd Infantry Brigade Brigadier N.I. Whitty
2nd Battalion The Royal Sussex Regiment
4th Battalion The Royal Sussex Regiment
5th Battalion The Royal Sussex Regiment

Artillery Brigadier E.P.H. Pease Watkin
57th Field Regiment, RA
58th Field Regiment, RA
65th Field Regiment, RA
57th (East Surrey) Anti-Tank Regiment, RA

Royal Engineers Lieutenant-Colonel B.T. Godfrey-Faussett
11th Field Company
208th Field Company
210th Field Company
211th Field Park Company

Appendix F ~ Special Operation Order, 21 May 1940

URGENT AND CONFIDENTIAL.

To Officer Commanding,
225 Bty.
226 Bty.
227 Bty.
228 Bty.

EME/94.

----

21 May 40.

To:- 2nd-in-Command. For information.

Events in the last 24 hours have proved that it is necessary for me to clearly define the role of our Regiment in its present position.

(1) All guns have now been sited on the ground, and in these positions the 57th Anti-Tank Regiment will fight to the "LAST man and the LAST round."

(2) No gun will be withdrawn from its position unless orders are given by:- The Battery Commander ONLY.
Orders will be given only in this event of:-
(a) We are preparing to advance against the enemy.
(b) We are withdrawing to a more favourable position, either as a Troop, Battery, or Regiment. In this case orders will be given to the Battery Commander by the Commanding Officer.

Every single gun position is thought to be in the best position, and it is the solemn duty of gun commanders now to dig their guns in so as to withstand all attempts by the enemy to put the gun out of action, either by shell, bomb, or small arms fire.

Because a gun position is shelled, bombed, or fired at by small arms fire, is no reason at all why any gun should be withdrawn.

(Signed) R.L. Travers.

In the Field.

Lieut. Colonel, R.A.
Commanding 57th Anti-Tank Regt. R.A.

Appendix G ~ Brief Notes

The Anti-Tank Regiment in 1940

The strength of an anti-tank regiment was some 540 officers and men under the command of a Lieutenant-Colonel. A regiment consisted of a headquarters and four batteries each of 12 anti-tank guns, i.e. a total of 48. The batteries were divided into three troops each of four guns, and a troop into two sections of two guns.

The batteries were linked together by the regimental headquarters, which was also responsible for maintaining communications with higher command and for organising all aspects of administration, maintenance and resupply of the unit. A signals section with its wireless sets and dispatch riders, and the medical officer and his regimental aid post were usually sited with the headquarters.

The vehicles that carried the ammunition, petrol, rations and other necessities were organised into a B Echelon under the control of the Regimental Quartermaster.

Each battery, commanded normally by a Major, was a self-contained unit with its own administrative resources and therefore capable of independent employment. In action it would normally be placed under command of one of the infantry brigades in the division.

A Subaltern (Lieutenant or Second-Lieutenant) commanded a troop, although in the early war years it might also have been a Troop Sergeant Major.

An individual gun detachment of five men was usually commanded by a Sergeant or Bombardier (Corporal). The crew consisted of the gun commander, the loader, the layer (who aimed and fired the gun under the orders of the gun commander), and two ammunition numbers. An additional member of a detachment was the driver of the gun tower.

The regiment was fully mobilised so that it could move rapidly to meet the threat of an attack. In a defensive position the guns would be carefully sited, as part of a co-ordinated plan, to protect the infantry and other arms against tank attack. In the offensive the guns would be pushed forward to provide support and to consolidate the ground gained against an enemy counter attack.

The 2-pounder anti-tank gun

As its name suggests, the 2-pounder (pdr) anti-tank gun was specifically designed to pierce the armour of tanks and other armoured fighting vehicles. It was a direct fire weapon (i.e. the target is visible from the gun) firing a shell of high velocity with a flat trajectory. Its effective range was 2000 yards, but better results could be expected at 800 yards or less.

The gun was mounted on a low carriage with two wheels that could be quickly removed to enable the carriage to be lowered onto three legs for the normal firing method. Where time permitted a gun emplacement would be dug and the position concealed. In the case of an emergency, the gun could be fired from off its wheels, but the traverse was limited due to the main shield fouling the wheels.

While the 2-pdr was a good gun, it soon became outdated and was replaced by the heavier 6-pdr anti-tank gun.

Divisions, Corps and Armies

The division is the basic fighting element of all arms in the army. An infantry division normally consisted of three infantry brigades, each of three battalions, complete with its own artillery, engineers, communications and logistic support. See Appendix E for the order of battle of 44th (Home Counties) Infantry Division in 1940.

The anti-tank regiment was part of the divisional artillery, which also consisted of three field regiments equipped with the 25 pdr field gun. All were under the Commander Royal Artillery (CRA) of the division, who held a brigadier's rank.

A number of divisions would be grouped into a corps and the corps into an army. 44th Division was part of III Corps in the British Expeditionary Force (BEF).

Appendix H ~ Sources

War Diaries

The relevant files for the 57th Anti-Tank Regiment at The National Archives in Kew are WO 166/1630 (September 1939-March 1940), WO167/584 (April-May 1940) and WO167/603 for 228 Battery in April 1940. The Surrey History Centre in Woking holds a substitute war diary for 227 Battery covering the crucial dates 15-30 May 1940. Many of the divisional, brigade and unit diaries for 44 Infantry Division were also consulted. Extracts from the diaries are Crown copyright.

Published works

Bastin, Jeremy, The Norfolk Yeomanry in Peace and War 1782-1961(65 Anti-Tank Regiment), Fakenham 1986

Blaxland, Gregory, Destination Dunkirk, London 1973

Brown, John, In Durance Vile, London 1981

Breithaupt, Hans, Die Geschichte der 30. Infanterie-Division, 1939-1945, Bad Nauheim

Chaplin, Lieut-Colonel H.D., The Queen's Own Royal West Kent Regiment 1920-1950, London 1954

Courtney, Joseph H., Ubique, Privately Published

Ellis, Major L.F., The War in France & Flanders 1939-40, London 1953

Fazan, Colonel E.A.C., Cinque Ports Battalion (5 Royal Sussex), Chichester 1971

Foster, Major R.C.G., History of the Queen's Royal Regiment 1924-1948, Aldershot 1953

Fraser, David, And We Shall Shock Them, London 1983

Gawthorpe, Brig. J.B., 137 Infantry Brigade, A Formation of the T.A. in the First Year of the War, 1939-40 in Ça Ira, The Journal of The West Yorkshire Regiment

Guttery, D.R., The Queen's Own Worcestershire Hussars 1922-1956 (53 Anti-Tank Regiment), Stourbridge 1958

Hadley, Peter, Third Class to Dunkirk, A Worm's-Eye View of the B.E.F.,

1940, London 1944
Hughes, Maj. Gen. B.P., History of The Royal Regiment of Artillery, Between the Wars 1919-1939, London 1992
Knight, Colonel C.R.B., Historical Records of The Buffs 1919-1948, London 1951
Martineau, G.D., A History of The Royal Sussex Regiment, Chichester 1955
Pemberton, Brigadier A.L., The Development of Artillery Tactics and Equipment, The War Office 1951
Scott Daniell, David, History of The East Surrey Regiment 1920-1952, London 1957
Stanley Clarke Major E.B. and Tillott, Major A.T., From Kent to Kohima (4 West Kent), Aldershot 1951
The Editor, The Journal of The East Surrey Regiment, Kingston on-Thames 1920-1939
Various authors. Territorial Battalions of the Regiments of Surrey and their Successors, Guildford 1992
Weidinger, Otto. Das Reich II, 1940-1941, Winnipeg 1995. Translated by Bo Friesen
Wimbledon Boro' News 1938-1940

GENERAL INDEX (Chapters 2-10)

INDEX OF UNITS (CHAPTERS 2-10)

Printed by ProCo, Sheffield
www.procoprint.co.uk